A Long Continual Argument

The Selected Poems of John Newlove

A Long Continual Argument

The Selected Poems of John Newlove

Edited by Robert McTavish
With an Afterword by Jeff Derksen

CHAUDIERE BOOKS

Ottawa 2007

A Long Continual Argument
The Selected Poems of John Newlove

Cover design by Tanya Sprowl
Layout by Jennifer Mulligan
Edited for the press by Robert McTavish

printed and bound in Canada
by Custom Printers, Renfrew, Ontario

Chaudiere Books
858 Somerset Street West
Main Floor
Ottawa, Ontario
K1R 6R7

www.chaudierebooks.com
email: info@chaudierebooks.com

Library and Archives Canada Cataloguing in Publication

Newlove, John, 1938-2003.
A long continual argument : the selected poems of John Newlove / Robert McTavish, editor.

Includes index.
ISBN 978-0-9781601-9-7

I. McTavish, Robert, 1970- II. Title.

PS8527.E82A6 2007 C811'.54 C2007-905227-4

The collecting of poetry from one's experience as one goes along is not the same thing as merely writing poetry.

The poet makes silk dresses out of worms.

-Wallace Stevens

TABLE OF CONTENTS

Editor's Preface - by Robert McTavish 11

From GRAVE SIRS, 1961

Birds, Dear, 15

From ELEPHANTS, MOTHERS & OTHERS, 1963

The End Justifies the Means 16
The Arrival 17
My Daddy Drowned 18
Before the Big Bend Highway 19
Not Moving 20
Veregin 22
Funeral 23
No Furniture for a Room 24
White Cat 25

From MOVING IN ALONE, 1965

Then, If I Cease Desiring 26
Nothing is to be Said 27
For Judith, Now About Ten Years Old 28
Four Small Scars 30
In Libya 31
The Flowers 32
The Singing Head 35
Kamsack 37
East from the Mountains 38
In the Forest 40
The Well-Travelled Roadway 42
By the Church Wall 43
A Letter to Larry Sealey, 1962 45
Two Letters from Austria 47
Love Letter 48

You Know 49
That's the Way Everything Is 49
Vancouver Spring 50
Veregin, Moving in Alone 52
Three Days is Too Long 55

From BLACK NIGHT WINDOW, 1968

Black Night Window 56
North America 57
The Common Root 60
You Cannot Step Twice 61
The Crab Apples 62
The Dog 63
The Old Man 65
The Hitchhiker 66
Crazy Riel 67
Ride Off Any Horizon 69
Indian Women 74
The Double-Headed Snake 76
When I Heard of the Friend's Death 78
A Film of Lhasa 79
It Was All There 80
Lady, Lady 81
What Do You Want? 82
Public Library 83
No Song 87
Like a Canadian 88
The Squirrel Peanut Butter Song 89
Solitaire 91
The Mirror 92
Samuel Hearne in Wintertime 93
The Big Bend 96
The Pride 100

From THE CAVE, 1970

The Flower 107
The Engine and the Sea 108
Warm Wind 110
The Wind 111
Doukhobor 112
The Prairie 114
Before Sleep 115
Revenge 116
By the Grey Atlantic 117
God Bless You 117
Remembering Christopher Smart 118
America 119
Alcazar 120
How the Weather Is 121
The Apparition 123
The Fat Man 124
The Cave 130

From LIES, 1972

And the Dead Rose up from the Water 131
Every Muddy Road 132
The Hero Around Me 133
The Sky 134
My Dreams 135
White Lies 136
Slow Spring 137
Company 138
Crow Walking 144
Gross Masks 146
It Is a City 147
No Pleasure 148
She 149
Notes From and Among the Wars 151
Like a River 160

The First Bird of Spring 161
Until It Was Yellow 162
Dream 163
Dream 163
Complaint 164
Everywhere I Go 164
Why Do You Hate Me? 165
Blue Cow Phrases 166
In the Crammed World 167
A Long Continual Argument With Myself 169

From THE GREEN PLAIN, 1979

The Green Plain 170

From THE NIGHT THE DOG SMILED, 1986

Driving 175
The Cities We Longed For 176
The Permanent Tourist Comes Home 178
Rocks, Woods, Seas 180
Concerning Stars, Flowers, Love, Etc. 181
Big Mirror 182
Yukichi Fukuzawa 185
Return Train 186
Like Water 186
Report on Absence 187
Svejk 188
Cold, Heat 189
Shakespeare's Sonnets 190
Insect Hopes 191
Five Poems After Sanskrit 194
Speech About a Blackfoot Woman With Travois, Photo By R.H. Trueman 196
White Philharmonic Novels 197
The Weather 207

From APOLOGY FOR ABSENCE, 1993

Being Caught 208
Autobiography 211
Autobiography 211
God Bless the Bear 212
Autobiography 213
Autobiography 213
Poem with Ravens 214
Such Fun, Such Fun 215
Autobiography 216
Progress 217

From THE TASMANIAN DEVIL & Other Poems, 1999

Fifty-Seventh Birthday 227
Love Affair 228
An Old Man, Waiting 228
An Examination 229
The Cat 230
A Picture From An Exhibition 230
It's Winter in Ottawa 231
Home Town 232
A Cartoon 233
Like an Eel 234
An Inscription To Richard Jeffries on a Sarsen at Barbury 235

From GROUNDSWELL: the best of above/ground press, 2003

The Death of the Hired Man 236

"These Things Form Poems When I Allow It": After John Newlove by Jeff Derksen 237

Index of Titles 246

Acknowledgements 250

Editor's Preface

Robert McTavish

> "Myself, I listen and read and watch. Phrases come into my mind, usually more interesting for their rhythms than for what they say, and sometimes they can ignite an entire set of rhythms, poetic, dramatic, horizontal (the line), perpendicular (the stanza and the whole piece), and at the same time it becomes important that I find the meaning of what is being said as well and make it as plain as I can. Sometimes it is not plain at all; sometimes there remains a shimmering or a veil or a hint of magic about which it is impossible to be more explicit. I can only approach it as closely as my craft or art allow me; then it must be left to itself. In the meantime, a lifetime accumulates characteristic rhythms and vocabularies and shapes in the mind to, at least in part, allow the would-be poet to make a poem. "Makar" (maker) was the Scots word for a poet."

John Newlove wasn't one to theorize much in print. He was, as critic WJ Keith noted, much more interested in making poems than being a poet. The above statement, in response to a young writer seeking advice, is but one example of the pathologically shy man as polite, engaging, and generous in isolation.

As an isolated reader I was first attracted to Newlove's consolation that one wasn't alone in the confusing maw. His was less a voice of reason than one able to confidently describe his bad tidings, simultaneously plainspoken and intelligent. Whether calmly bathing in "the sea-going garbage/ of civilization" or wanting a lover who "suffers indignities willingly," for me Newlove's work is always memorable, and often unforgettable. The ideas he engages with at any moment yield to the sound of the words themselves. These poems are the markers of the life of his mind.

I first interviewed John in 1998. By then he had withdrawn from the literary world, content to read alone and on occasion write. Tucked away inside his high walls of books I found him self-deprecating and sly, his low tone punctuated with cigarette pauses. In that interview I learned fragments of the life that ran parallel to the poems.

Born in 1938, a child in Saskatchewan moves hamlet to hamlet with his schoolteacher mother. Later, his lawyer father back on the wagon, his parents reunited, an intelligent, bored teen drinks to alleviate boredom and insecurity in his small prairie town. A penniless hitchhiker is adrift on the highway, or lost in a book in the public library. A poet writes, a young family and the spectre of absent money about him. The ebb and flow of depression and alcoholism. The poems keep coming.

There is really
not so much to learn

after all: roll with the punch,
prepare for the next dumb blow.

from "You Cannot Step Twice"

A sampling of titles from early critical assessments sets the tone: *Something in which to believe for once, More than just honest despair, How do I get out of here?* John himself would state in his preface to *The Green Plain* that most of his writing stemmed from "the real knowledge of the existence of a veritable paradise and the real knowledge of the tiny monster, the ogre, lurking like a shadow in the greenness." Yet while a dry, vicious wit and lyricism may not counter certain self-conscious, destructive urges in the work, the musicality of much of Newlove's work lends elegance to an otherwise dark vision. The low, cadenced voice amidst the chaos is making the syntax heard. Craftily rolling with the punches, Newlove is the cork in his Heraclitian water, weathering it all. Throughout his work he appreciates the small, if dubious, victories; the "moments, not monuments;" the potential tastes of honey. It will be a long continual argument.

A writer produces four books and four chapbooks in a tumultuous decade. An editor/poet with a major publisher wins his country's highest poetry award but the workload and notoriety become too much. Despite writer residencies and grants, he finds it difficult to write, his demons easy to embrace. His only other full book comes 14 years later, after easing into a stable home in Ottawa. A self-imposed exile. Small poems still come as if bits of a peeling fresco, their relationships unclear:

LIKE AN EEL

Hunting after myself in slightly used poems
is a heartbreaking chore. The past
is a foreign country and the quarry

is sly and elusive, a liar twisting
and twisting about the words like an eel
on a spear, dying, never to be known.

Newlove was obsessed with lies. His poems accept the imperfection, the ability to lie inherent in art, often approaching with sardonic humour or a sober tone his disappointment and disillusion with the ways of the world. He writes in pursuit of the ideal through this imperfect means (In *Lies* he quotes the *Commentaries of Pius II*: "Lies and perjury were so familiar/ to him that he often deceived/ himself and told the truth when he/ thought he was lying."). As with Wallace Stevens before him, he sees the poet as "maker," though the world he makes is doomed in relation to "the world as it is." Yet right up to the debilitating stroke that would lead to his death two years later at age 65, John continued what was now a hardscrabble pursuit of poems: "I'd still like to throw them one high hard one," he told me. On the page he lived a second reality, a second life. His complicated argument – conducted alone – is never resolved, but for the reader it makes room for conjecture and pleasure. It is little, but it is little enough.

This collection includes all of the poems from Newlove's previous Selected Poems with 37 more to allow for the full range and scope of his work. Here is the arc of a stellar career that moved from almost documentary origins to a larger vision where dreams and pieces of history real and imagined, public and personal, coalesce as poetry. The prodigious 60's loner persona, so wicked with his love in the influential *Moving in Alone*. *Black Night Window*'s history-steeped poet of the "places I adhere and live in," his interpretation enmeshed in an era's cultural nationalism. The sheer bleakness and knifepoint majesty of *Lies*. The later contemplations and their eventual compression into echoes, questions, statements; an argument winding down.

I would see other sides of John, but his frankness, energy, and delight that first night were a marvel: the maker of poems. Leaving that initial interview, five hours later, I turned in the doorway to see him laughing sheepishly, both his hands forming a gunfighter's guns: "When he's been solitary, one comes at you with both barrels."

From GRAVE SIRS, 1961

BIRDS, DEAR,

birds, dear, fly by not moving: the wings
balance each other: when you shoot them
they will continue to coast

they too make their circles, large at first,
then smaller: eventually they land:
be patient: I love you.

From ELEPHANTS, MOTHERS & OTHERS, 1963

THE END JUSTIFIES THE MEANS

The end does not
justify the means, there is no end.
The means are not justified or
unjustified, they exist.

The meanings are not justified
or unjustified, exist
in you. The meanness
is not justified or unjustified,

is. Is in you, exists, and
around you. Means
and a meaning, go round you, to no end.

THE ARRIVAL

Having come slowly, hesitantly
at first, as a poem comes,
and then steadily down to the marshy seaboard:

that day I ran along the stone sea-break,
plunging into the Pacific, the sun
just setting, clothed, exuberant, hot,
so happy –
                    o sing!
plunging into the ocean, rolled on my back, eyes
full of salt water, hair in eyes,
shoes lost forever at the bottom, noting
as if they were trivia
the wheeling birds of the air
and gulls gorging themselves
on the sea-going garbage
of civilization, the lower mainland,
hauled away by tugs –
                                        they,
being too heavy to fly,
and foolish-looking there,
can be knocked off with sticks
from barge into ocean –

and noting the trees whitely flowering,
took off my clothes and calmly bathed.

MY DADDY DROWNED

My daddy drowned still blind kittens
in the rainbarrel corner of our white house
& I make poems babies & love-affairs
out of women I've only seen once

or maybe never at all. Daddy
had to push those kittens under in a sack
to keep them from squealing & I don't know
whether he hated or enjoyed it; no expression

was permitted to cross his legal face. I'm
the same way, Freud says so, I let
no expression on my lips when I read,

pushing those women underneath
to drown in poems. It's one way
to get them down. But I wonder about daddy,
if he's the same as me,
                                        because sometimes
I let those women slip to the surface
& squeak a little bit before I kill them.

BEFORE THE BIG BEND HIGHWAY

I stand on the west corner of that road
(going the opposite way this time)
outside Revelstoke, watching the hoods
drive back and forth, dangerously,
the same oiled quartets each time,
eyeing and laughing: I consider the night
just passed, spent nearly in rain,
partly in cold and windy showers before
the downpour, then how the rest of it
went in the dark cabin
                                        of that mad old man,
flopped on the wooden floor,
deliciously at his insistence
reading Ezekiel to him, Ezekiel
whom he loved, Ezekiel who prophesied,
he said, The End Of The World,
deeply rolling the rhetorical syllables,
the allegory of Gog....

NOT MOVING

Waterfalls
in the dark
& the noise

very much

        the animals
        undoubtedly
        moving there
        & waiting

rocks
rolling down
the gravel
cuts
of the road

        there
        bears be
        pack rats (curious
        to see) snakes
        lizards

deer moving
among
the trees
quietly

also
on the side
of the road
me

smoking
nervously
at midnight
100 miles
to go

& cold
& afraid
on the side of the road

the only animal

not moving
at all.

VEREGIN

The pure white bodies of my friends,
d'un blanc pur, like –
like a cigarette paper! shivering

in cold spring before a cold
shallow waterhole. Thin naked
bodies, ribs, knees, buttocks, hearts,

young bilingual doukhobors,
where are you now? I cut my foot
on a piece of rusty tin and walked
home alone, shoe full of blood.

FUNERAL

So she said to me, my
mother that is, or
whoever you like, riding
out to the cemetery in the

slow rain, the comfortable car,
she said, Don't
cry, don't show them anything, don't,
don't let them see it,

and the priest stood there, who
later died of cancer, and
was so mild, coughing
prayers in his black cassock

(and what my uncle said is
a different matter), she
said, Don't expose yourself,
don't let them laugh.

NO FURNITURE FOR A ROOM

The obnoxiously generated
neon suspense of bingo next door.

The entombing buses slide by
to a non-varying end.

No furniture for a room, excepting
the varnished desk and the grey mattress –
walls pink, protruding doors, corners,
and angles, dissonances,
everywhere: bad shadows at night.

And out on the wet September streets
orange berries on the grey sidewalk.

Light coats pressed against their thighs
the bodies of beautiful women walk by.

WHITE CAT

I like orange juice
better than anything else
in the world, she said –
wearing a blue dress;

when I wrote it down,
drinking cold tapwater she
turned and, What
did you do? said, then

came, sat in
the rocker chair, picked
up the small white cat,
said, This cat is

sick, John, do you think
she has distemper? And
when I said, How should
I know, she touched

the cat again, held it
up, regarding the eye
it had injured weeks earlier,
said, Is it? Is it?

From MOVING IN ALONE, 1965

THEN, IF I CEASE DESIRING

Then, if I cease desiring,
you may sing a song
of how young I was.

You may praise famous moments,
all have them, of the churches
I broke into for wine,

not praise, the highways
I travelled drunkenly
in winter, the cars I stole.

You may allow me moments,
not monuments, I being
content. It is little,
but it is little enough.

NOTHING IS TO BE SAID

Everything ends once
and cannot be recovered,
even our poor selves.

Your tongue thrusts into my mouth
violently and I am lost,
nothing is to be said. I am plunged
into the black gap again.

It is not to be endured
easily, unthought of, never
to be dismissed with ease.

What can I do. My hand
shakes on the page. Knowing
I am criminality, there is
nothing I dare do.

Ah, I can't go home
and make love to her either,
pretending it's you.

FOR JUDITH, NOW ABOUT TEN YEARS OLD

Judith, niece, red
welted scars on
your not yet
adolescent chest,

slits cut, say,
yearly, so you
may lift your arms,

welt ridges also
on the not even yet
about to be

womanly posterior
from where
the failing grafts
were taken, girl

who pulled down
on your birthday, I
think I remember,

the scalding water
from the black,
polished, wood-burning
stove, screaming,

so young, perhaps
ten now, years after,
do you remember
the prairie town

you were ruined in,
can you recall
the smell of it,
the smell you had?
What will you do
when your breasts come?

I don't know. I remember
the feel of your tough
rubber-laced skin
as I spread salve on it.

FOUR SMALL SCARS

This scar beneath my lip
is symbol of a friend's rough love
though some would call it anger,
mistakenly. This scar

crescent on my wrist
is symbol of a woman's delicate anger
though some would call it love,
mistakenly. My belly's scar

is symbol of a surgical precision:
no anger, no love. The small
fading mark on my hand

is token of my imprecision,
of my own carving, my anger and my love.

IN LIBYA

I was in libya
with jason & there
wrote a poem of it, a bad one

being numbed by
all that death
& the death to come, young
to be slaughtered:

a bad way to write
poems, & I was in syracuse
when lamachos died & the army died

later & it was said, These,
having done what men could, suffered
what men must: & wrote a poem of it
& poems of all the deaths to come.

THE FLOWERS

It is raining, rain
streaks down the window to my left,
cars sluice water in the gutters
in the night, the round
neon clock-containing sign
hanging outside beside my window
sways in the wind and buzzes.

The flowers sprout everywhere,
in pots and boxes, on lawns
and trees, in gardens and ditches
the flowers are growing; the wet
wind will nourish them, cut
some down but feed the rest.

The sign crackles
and swings on its bar,
iron bar; the cars go by
all the night. They cut
a momentary trail and mark,
disappearing, on the wet
black pavement. The cars go by,
the police in their cars
prowl restlessly
up and down the rainy avenue
looking for interlopers, anyone
afoot at night in the rain,
the blue and dangerous
gun-hipped cops.

The car came smashing
and wrecking his face, his head,
poor hit hurt head
bleeding on the roadway
and in the cool hospital
night in bandages
and glued-on tape.

His eyes, they said,
were soft and easy
years ago. Now
he wears them cleverly
like some secret
coupled badge,
twin and original, dark
ice eyes that watch and assess
slowly what they have
fixed
on; his head does not move.

In the hospitals
with antiseptic nurses
stripping him, knife-
fisted surgeons bending down,

they cut, irony,
to save his life; and he stayed
days and years filled
with tantalizing drugs, interminable
dreams, tangled in bandages and
shocks, suspicions, a nonchalant
profusion of hopes and cures,
surrounded by the tears
of his rainy crazy peers.

Rain, wind, and spring, all things
drove him crazy and grow
flowers, flowers
that dance in the rain,
the bulging flowers that grew
in his head, plants
of evil or god, some
holy epileptic angel, bloated
inhuman flowers shining
their bright colours
insistently, turning
slowly in the wind
and spring, tortuous
creaking growths, thick
cancerous things
in the rain, stems
like the barrels of rifles,
fat lead bullet roots
gripping the damp earth.

And the cars
pass up and down
the streets, disappearing
trails, the blue police
pass, coughing
behind their leathery fists,
guns dangling
from their hips, eyes
watching. My flowery clock
buzzes and mutters,
typewriter taps
like the rain. I breathe
as harshly as the wind.

THE SINGING HEAD

The singing head that
does not falter when
it falls

but sings for seven
short years more, or nine,

or for as long
as it may be lucky
to shout out the words
in measured time

or to the ear's delight
to hear

the auditory
nerves carry on
the sound,

the self-made sound
the mouth manufactured

of the air,
of the endless
chant of praised delight

that could
not feel the sword or
cry to feel its hot
blood gush

where the neck had led
to the caroling lungs
and balanced body tilting

in the wind, the head
in grass or just

tossed under any bush
or muddled in a ditch…

it carries on
to raise its breathless voice,
to praise

the life that while it lived
was good, to praise
the grass
or bush or muddy ditch,

that where it stays
is good.

KAMSACK

Plump eastern saskatchewan river town,
where even in the depression it's said the wheat
went thirty bushels and was full-bodied,
the river laying good black dirt each year:
but I found it arid, as young men will.

EAST FROM THE MOUNTAINS

The single, faltering, tenuous line of melody
displayed by a thin man's lungs
unsurely, halting in the winter air:

what to say? Oh, say nothing.
But listen to the blowing snow
at the house's wooden corner,
listen to the misery in the sound of the wind.

On a single wind, followed
by lonely silence, the snow
goes by. Outside
everything is gone; the white
sheer land answers no questions,
but only exists

as it ought to, the sun
shines now as it ought to shine,
shedding no warmth:
what to say.

To listen to the high-pitched wind
in winter removes the idea of hills,
makes clear the real geometry
of the land: east from the mountains
and east to the giant lakes and the river
no single distinction to ruin
the total wholeness of sweep
of the earth, untouched by the lights
of the cold and isolate cities:

following the tentative line
of a gully, it becomes lost at last
as in Qu'Appelle; following
the tentative line of the railway,
it gathers together and disappears;
the perspective is textbook,
the rare protuberance never in mind.

The cities do not extend to each other,
the hamlets exist alone,
the suspicious basses of voices
of farmers mutter in the horse-
urined yards, the wives and the children
wait for the spring, summer, fall, the grass,
the quick, unlasting reprieve, gone

like that! – and so hard
to hear what someone is saying:
it is important and real, what is said,
in the thrown-together town,
but is heard from a long way away,
hollow or shrill, and heard
with trouble. So hard

to attend as the issuing words
emerge from an icy tunnel of lung,
faltering, tenuous melody –

o tired and halting song!

IN THE FOREST

In the forest
down the cut roads
the sides of them
gravel rolls
thundering down,
each small stone
a rock waterfall
that frightens me
sitting in my ditch.

I smoke my last
cigarette rolled
with bible paper,
listen to the stone
casting down,
some of it bouncing
off my hunched shoulders.
Above me the dark grass
hangs over the edge
like a badly-fitted wig –
10 feet above me.

I dream of the animals
that may sulk there,
deer snake and bear
dangerous and inviolable
as I am not inviolable.
Even the gentle deer
scare me at midnight,
no one else for 100 miles,
even the sucking snakes
small and lithe as syrup.
The forest is not silent,
water smashes its way,
rocks bounce, wind magnifies

its usual noise
and my shivering fear
makes something alive
move in the trees,
shift in the grass
10 feet above me.

I am too frightened
to move or to stay,
sweating in the wind.
An hour later
I convulse unthinking,
and run, run, run down the cold road.

THE WELL-TRAVELLED ROADWAY

The dead beast, turned up
(brown fur on back and white
on the belly), lay on the roadway,
its paws extended in the air.

It was beautiful on the well-travelled roadway
with its dead black lips: God help me,
I did not even know what it was.
I had been walking into the city then,
early, with my own name in mind.

BY THE CHURCH WALL

The mocking faces appear in the churchyard,
appear as I curl on the hard ground
trying to sleep – trying to sleep
as the voices call me, asking why
must I always be frightened and dreaming?

I have traveled this road many times,
though not in this place, tired
in the bones and the long blistered feet,
beneath a black mass of flat clouds,
dry in a damned and useless land.

Frogs croak hollowly, the loons cry
their thin bewildered song on a far-off lake,
the wind rises and the wet grass waves;
by the wall of the white rural church
I count a thousand to go to sleep.

But it will not happen. The faces
float before me, bloated and grinning,
succubus and incubus, a child
screams in a house across the road;
I turn and turn in my fear.

There is nothing to hurt me here,
and I know it, but an ancient dread
clenches my belly and fluttering heart,
and in the cold wet grass I count
what may happen and what has.

All the mistakes and desires are here,
old nameless shame for my lies,
and the boy's terrible wish to be good and
not to be alone, not to be alone,
to be loved, and to love.

I remember a letter a friend sent,
trivial and gossiping, quite plain,
of no consequence to him, casually typed
and then signed easily by hand,
All our love, and wish I could say that.

But I lie alone in the shadowed grass,
fond only, incapable of love or truth,
caught in all I have done, afraid
and unable to escape, formulating
one more ruinous way to safety.

A LETTER TO LARRY SEALEY, 1962.

November 15th.

Gone past Hope, through Hell's Gate and the China Bar,
around the rock dynamite slides, in
with the timorous driver going 45 in 60-zones,
he is unable to eat, complaining about his new false teeth,
how they hurt him and cut his gums, me,
having sold at last my typewriter
after having tried to give it away
unsuccessfully, books, letters, poems,
shirts, stories, lies, mirrors, shoes and my cowboy hat,
all given into the hands of friends
for use or for keeping, I have arrived
in Cache Creek, on the way
to Edmonton, spending my little money
on hotel beds, bread and beef,
necessary comforts before the lull,
stopping too soon, unable to sleep, think,
relax, waiting for morning and the movement
to begin again.

November 16th, 730am.

Awakened in rain by the rap of the soft-woolen-
sweater-breasted desk-girl, she
only a wooden door away from naked me,
I shower and shave, dress, descend the stairs
for coffee, all I dare buy, and the road,
sleeping-bag rolled under an arm,
observing how my sound
becomes more sensual, and thicker, on the road,
as the prospects diminish,
how the commas and hyphens abound.

And 900am.

After coffee, Sail Along Silv'ry Moon playing,
Billy Vaughn, quick rides through Kamloops, Chase,
Salmon Arm, Canoe, then short ones
past Sicamous and other unnamable towns
lazily until an ancient half-ton truck
took me to Revelstoke where the new highway
is, no more Big Bend and its rocks.
                                        Five minutes after,
the first salesman's car, Calgary by eight
and a safe paid room in the Sally Ann.

November 17th.

Buying a pack for the clumsy bag,
zoomed to Edmonton, north, the Hostel, to beds,
to breakfast mush and supper, bummed cigarettes,
sitting dull-eyed day-long in the railway station.
Edmonton. November. Cold. Snow. I am sitting
on the edge of the bed, scribbling on paper towels,
afraid of the ostentation; broke, tired, happy.

TWO LETTERS FROM AUSTRIA

Out of any thing at hand, once
out of three hungry days
in the bush, spider-devilled and scared,
trotting down the woodsy roads at midnight,
woods dreamed full of bears
as Granville Street with cops, even the deer
dangerous, wrapped in death; once
out of a single glass of cider,
other things numerously crowding in,
poems are begun. And now
a pair of letters, not even new,
from a barely-known girl in Austria.

You say, serious girl, Sorry for this weak
green effort. But names of places
are three feet deep in these letters, made
real by your excited presence in them;
these things form poems when I allow it.

Oh no, I'm not in love with you, or will be.
It's too easy to fall in love by letter,
at long distance too many things
may be ignored. But your letters
make me real in one more mind and make places
briefly more real for me. I can fill up poems
with them. And since
you are smarter than I am and know
this act of writing is an act of love,
although you do not love me either,
you sign your letters: Love.

LOVE LETTER

How are you? And whose
hero do you want me
to be. My tooth hurts

and it is raining, there is
no oil for the stove.
Or when there is

it leaks on the floor.
Is your father well?
I'm spitting

blood again, from
that abscessed tooth
I always suck on.

And how is your father:
that bastard I've never met.
And your mother.

Goddamn them both. I hope
I never meet them. Or
you again. Love.

YOU KNOW

You know I can't talk
when all that goes on.

Would you have me lie
to please you?

I can not lie. I would,
to please you.

THAT'S THE WAY EVERYTHING IS

That's the way everything is now,
sweetheart. And we are too.

Beat to hell and we love it. Not
beatitude. Tired. Too tired

to find a handkerchief. You litter
the bed with little bits of toilet paper.

I litter the bed with toilet paper too.
Have a cigarette. Or go to sleep, you.

VANCOUVER SPRING

City in a cold paranoiac acetylene-light dawn
slowly warming up
with gulls in the water
gulls in the air
gulls on the buildings
pigeons and eagles in the air
sparrows and neon in the air
hawks
rain and fog in the air
smell of it
the white-and-
brown-streaked statues of minor men
or soldiers making european flowers now
parks and parking lots
gun-hipped policemen
in brass badges
blue uniforms
black and
prowling cars with red lights
sirens
handcuffs
and gas waiting to be used
the patina'd statues worn green in the rain
art galleries and other butcher shops
heaving concrete sidewalks
and carefully
heaving-breathing
javex blondes with real wire brassieres
marking and lifting them
sailors
bewildered old ladies
old ladies with strange hats
tall feathers
yanked from the rumps of old odd dead extinct birds
stuck in them
stuck in the hats

librarians and lawyers
longshoremen
and flowers
lit buses
making happy xylophone sounds on their wires
making happy
xylophone sounds in their full coinboxes
prostitutes with
their full coinboxes
busboys
sharp-cornered banks and evil blindmen tapping on them
with white canes and coins
cornered customers inside
tourists and whores and flowers
beer-waiters
taking taxis to work
evangelists
newspaper boxes
crippled newspapermen
slobbering on headlines
hunchback newspapermen in red wool
toques and torn scarves against the wind and rain
university students
adversity students
traffic lights
salesmen
cabbies
dozens of languages and thousands of tongues
to twist them
mouths to lip them –

standing in the light
here
things come –

birds: gulls: neon: police
rain
signs in the air.

VEREGIN, MOVING IN ALONE

fatherless, 250 people
counting dogs and gophers
we would say, Jmaeff's grocerystore,
me in grade 4, mother
principal of the 2-building
3-room 12-grade school.

a boy sitting on the grass
of a small hill, the hot fall,
speaking no russian, an airgun
my sister gave me making me envied.

I tried all fall, all spring
the next ominous year, to kill
a crow with it, secretly glad
I could not, the men
in winter shooting the town's
wild dogs, casually tossing
the quick-frozen, barely-bleeding
head-shot corpses onto
the street-side snowbanks,

the highway crews cutting their way
through to open the road with what
I was sure was simply
some alternate of a golden summer's
wheat-threshing machine, children
running through the hard-tossed spray,
pretending war from the monster's snout,

leaping into snowbanks
from Peter The Lordly Veregin's
palace on the edge of town
in a wild 3-dimensional
cubistic game of cops and robbers,

cold spring swimming
in Dead Horse Creek and farmers' dugouts
and doomed fishing
in beastless ponds, strapped
in school for watching a fight,

coldly holding back tears
and digging for drunken father's
rum-bottle, he had finally
arrived, how I loved him,
loved him, love him, dead, still.

My mad brother chased me
alone in the house with him
around and around
the small living room, airgun,
rifle in hand, silently
our breaths coming together –

all sights and temperatures
and remembrances,
as a lost gull screams now
outside my window,
a 9-year-old's year-long
night and day in tiny
magnificent prairie Veregin:

the long grey cat we got,
the bruised knees, cut fingers,
nails in feet, far walks
to watch a horse's corpse
turn slowly and sweetly to bone,
white bone, and in late spring
too, I remember the bright
young bodies of the boys,

my friends and peers and enemies
till everything breaks down.

THREE DAYS IS TOO LONG

When shall I see you again?
Three days is too long,
anything can happen, nothing
is so bad that it cannot get worse,
all things are spoilt
by my humourless viciousness,
my love. My love, my malicious
movement toward life
is so bad it cannot get worse:
my love, my love, my deliciously
hurting movement to life.

From BLACK NIGHT WINDOW, 1968

BLACK NIGHT WINDOW

Black night window –
rain running down
the fogged glass,

a blanched leaf
hanging outside
on a dead twig,

the moon dead,
the wind dying
in the trees,

in this valley,
in this recession.

NORTH AMERICA

The white wine
moves
in the crooked
glass.

It causes
curious
thought, curiosity,
a medley

of sounds
from other men's
tongues,
lost things

stolen
for savour
and profit, some
sort

of salvation
or peace
for a moment,
moving

the mind
away from a need
for wine
to

a disinterested
remembrance –
like a flower,
dried.

As: 'we rode
through
several thickets
composed

of nettles
and briars
so thickly
matted

together as
almost
to forbid
passage –

our horses
were
so torn that
the blood

streamed down
their legs and
breasts,'
is remembered:

through how
many hands
have
those words

come? – to me,
so
that the noise
made

of the continent
might be
recovered to
my mind.

THE COMMON ROOT

If you won't say
anything, then
shut up, the indian
whore in the cafe

said to me. What
could I say, now
she spoke, to show
that I had got

just what I wanted –
to sit silently
all the winter day
and not to be taunted

with friendly questions
proving me the outsider,
alone, unknowing, and her
surrounded by ones

she recognized or
understood without
knowing, the root
of common penury for

all of us the same,
but my practice astray
and my ancestry
shown in a strange name.

YOU CANNOT STEP TWICE

'You cannot step twice
into the same river,'
or twice

into the same disaster,
though the difference may be
only an atom's –

the hairbreadth
of a smile, a slight
turning away, the hand

running through the hair
in exasperation. There is really
not so much to learn

after all; roll with the punch,
prepare for the next dumb blow.

THE CRAB APPLES

I am creeping back into being
a poet again perhaps, the last

tentative lines have come to me
saying Why not? I tell you this spring

every two weeks or so, the dead branches
suddenly revivifying themselves with a grafted fruit

slightly different in nature each time, this
is a difficult approach, it makes ill-tempered waiting;

but even the wrinkled crab apple satisfies me –
in boyhood I stole them from a neighbour's tree.

THE DOG

Lying on my back
on the hot prairie
dreaming of
the nervous sea,

my .22 rifle
by my side, my dog
ranging about and snuffing,
content that I

should do nothing, for
he was a damn fool
of a dog, red and curly,
and always scared

away the crows or gophers
before I could shoot,
dreaming of the sea
and anything to do except

what was at hand
I spent the summers,
never thinking anyone
would love me,

never caring beyond
the delight at making
myself feel sad
and the false tears

tightening my throat
as I worked myself down,
never thinking anyone
could love me, not

as I loved myself – except
that red dog, damn fool
running and barking
away toward the town.

THE OLD MAN

The old man
in the sawdust yard
was no old man
but father

me the coward
skinny
10-year-old watching

the two others wave
their hammers
coming on –

later at supper
I blushed with love
hearing him tell
how he made them run!

THE HITCHHIKER

On that black highway,
where are you going? –

it is in Alberta
among the trees

where the road sweeps
left and right

in great concrete arcs
at the famous resort –

there you stood on
the road in the wind,

the cold wind going
through you and you

going through the country
to no end, only

to turn again at one sea
and begin it again,

feeling safe with strangers
in a moving car.

CRAZY RIEL

Time to write a poem
or something.
Fill up a page.
The creature noise.
Huge massed forces of men
hating each other.
What young men do not know.
To keep quiet,
contemporaneously.
Contempt. The robin diligently
on the lawn sucks up worms,
hopping from one to another.
Youthfully. Sixteen miles
from my boyhood home
the frogs sit in the grassy marsh
that looks like a golf course
by the lake. Green frogs.
Boys catch them for bait or sale.
Or caught them. Time.
To fill up a page.
To fill up a hole.
To make things feel better. Noise.
The noise of the images
that are people I will never understand.
Admire them though I may.
Poundmaker. Big Bear. Wandering Spirit,
those miserable men.
Riel. Crazy Riel. Riel hanged.
Politics must have its way.
The way of noise. To fill up.
The definitions bullets make,
and field guns.
The noise your dying makes,
to which you are the only listener.

The noise the frogs hesitate
to make as the metal hook
breaks through the skin
and slides smoothly into place
in the jaw. The noise
the fish makes caught in the jaw,
which is only an operation
of the body and the element,
which a stone would make
thrown in the same water, thrashing,
not its voice.
The lake is not displaced
with one less jackfish body.
In the slough that looks like a golf course
the family of frogs sings. Metal throats.
The images of death hang upside-down.
Grey music.
It is only the listening for death,
fingering the paraphernalia,
the noise of the men you admire.
And cannot understand.
Knowing little enough about them.
The knowledge waxing.
The wax that paves hell's road,
slippery as the road to heaven.
So that as a man slips
he might as easily slide
into being a saint as destroyer.
In his ears the noise magnifies.
He forgets men.

RIDE OFF ANY HORIZON

Ride off any horizon
and let the measure fall
where it may –

on the hot wheat,
on the dark yellow fields
of wild mustard, the fields

of bad farmers, on the river,
on the dirty river full
of boys and on the throbbing

powerhouse and the low dam
of cheap cement and rocks
boiling with white water,

and on the cows and their powerful
bulls, the heavy tracks
filling with liquid at the edge

of the narrow prairie
river running steadily away.

*

Ride off any horizon
and let the measure fall
where it may –

among the piles of bones
that dot the prairie

in vision and history
(the buffalo and deer,

dead indians, dead settlers,
the frames of lost houses

left behind in the dust
of the depression,

dry and profound, that
will come again in the land

and in the spirit, the land
shifting and the minds

blown dry and empty –
I have not seen it! except

in pictures and talk –
but there is the fence

covered in dust, laden,
the wrecked house stupidly empty) –

here is a picture for your wallet,
of the beaten farmer and his wife
leaning toward each other –

sadly smiling, and emptied of desire.

*

Ride off any horizon
and let the measure fall
where it may –

off the edge
of the black prairie

as you thought you could fall,
a boy at sunset

not watching the sun
set but watching the black earth,

never-ending they said in school,
round: but you saw it ending,

finished, definite, precise –
visible only miles away.

*

Ride off any horizon
and let the measure fall
where it may –

on a hot night the town
is in the streets –

the boys and girls
are practising against

each other, the men
talk and eye the girls –

the women talk and
eye each other, the indians
play pool: eye on the ball.

*

Ride off any horizon
and let the measure fall
where it may –

and damn the troops, the horsemen
are wheeling in the sunshine,
the cree, practising

for their deaths: mr poundmaker,
gentle sweet mr big bear,
it is not unfortunately

quite enough to be innocent,
it is not enough merely
not to offend –

at times to be born
is enough, to be
in the way is too much –

some colonel otter, some
major-general middleton will
get you, you –

indian. It is no good to say,
I would rather die
at once than be in that place –

though you love that land more,
you will go where they take you.

*

Ride off any horizon
and let the measure fall –

where it may;
it doesn't have to be

the prairie. It could be
the cold soul of the cities
blown empty by commerce

and desiring commerce
to fill up the emptiness.

The streets are full of people.

It is night, the lights
are on; the wind

blows as far as it may. The streets
are dark and full of people.

Their eyes are fixed as far as
they can see beyond each other –

to the concrete horizon, definite,
tall against the mountains,
stopping vision visibly.

INDIAN WOMEN

Saturday night
kamsack is
something
to lie about,

the streets full
of indians and
doukhobors,
raw men and

fat women (watch
out for
the women people
said, all the men

do is drink
beer and play
pool but watch
out for those

indian women),
cars
driving up
and down the

main street
from the new
high school

building to
the cn
station and
back

again, paved
road where
the rest were
only oiled

gravel in
the good
old summer

time, in the good
old summertime,
son, when
everybody who

was nobody was
out on the street
with a belly

full talking
to beat
hell and
the heat.

THE DOUBLE-HEADED SNAKE

Not to lose the feel of the mountains
while still retaining the prairies
is a difficult thing. What's lovely
is whatever makes the adrenalin run;
therefore I count terror and fear among
the greatest beauty. The greatest
beauty is to be alive, forgetting nothing,
although remembrance hurts
like a foolish act, is a foolish act.

Beauty's whatever
makes the adrenalin run. Fear
in the mountains at night-time's
not tenuous, it is not the cold
that makes me shiver, civilized man,
white, I remember
the stories of the Indians,
Sis-i-utl, the double-headed snake.

Beauty's what makes
the adrenalin run. Fear at night
on the level plains, with no horizon
and the stars too bright, wind bitter
even in June, in winter
the snow harsh and blowing,
is what makes me
shiver, not the cold air alone.

And one beauty cancels another. The plains
seem secure and comfortable
at Crow's Nest Pass; in Saskatchewan
the mountains are comforting
to think of; among
the eastwardly diminishing hills
both the flatland and the ridge
seem easy to endure.

As one beauty
cancels another, remembrance
is a foolish act, a double-headed snake
striking in both directions, but I
remember plains and mountains, places
I come from, places I adhere and live in.

WHEN I HEARD OF THE FRIEND'S DEATH

When I heard of the friend's death in the mechanized city,
who was so clever, so young, so pleasant, I was ashamed

to be alive, all my faults in me, and him spoiled,
dirty and unreasonable at the accident's will.

Just so it is horrible to think of my father on his dead back
in the box, packed under dirt, his handsome face

falling apart. How curiously we deceive ourselves.

There is no consolation to be had anywhere for this.
There is always so much more to be said than can be said.

A FILM OF LHASA

In the film shot by one of their brethren the monks move
with ease across an overexposed landscape. Dalai Lama
is going to three monasteries to pass his exams. It is the
first time I have seen a man almost a god moving.

The scattered bushes are light green on white soil, the
garments of the lesser men have been washed many
times.

All move slowly, chatting – no urgency when a man
becomes a god or part of a god. It is ordained, what will
happen; the perfect moments will be found. And exalted
the ordinances!

An emperor of Rome smiling on the deathbed
sardonically made a joke of his impending divinity. Dalai
Lama does not die; he smiles, moving back and forth, he
questions the examiners and claps his hands like a small
delighted boy.

IT WAS ALL THERE

I am now a servant only
of what in my innocence
I had wished to make myself.

Successful, I am unsuccessful; complete,
I am more empty than ever.

These compulsive trips
into the mountains
that frighten me, these runnings away –

what reputation do I have to make?

It was all there, all
the time, I could
sit back quietly now and nothing would change.

I have been too careful for that.
The stuttering boy
is known as the glib

obnoxious insulter, but alone
he still hems, picks up things left-handedly,
and cannot make an order.

LADY, LADY

Lady, lady, I cannot lie,
I didn't cut down your cherry tree.

It was another man, in another season,
for the same reason.

I eat the stone and not the flesh,
it is the bare bone of desire I want,

something you would throw a dog,
or me, though I insult by saying so.

God knows it is not said
of your body, that it is like

a bone thrown to a dog,
or that I would throw it away, which

moment to moment I cannot remember
under those baggy clothes you wear –

which, if I love and tell,
I love well.

WHAT DO YOU WANT?

I want a good lover
who will not mistreat me
and suffers indignities willingly;
who is so good in bed
she covers my faults and will claim
the skill's mine, and love me,
and gossip too
to enhance my sexual fame –

what do you want,
what do you want?

I want a good lover
who will cook good meals
and listen respectfully;
shine my shoes, back my lies
with invented statistics at parties;
suffer indignities willingly
and be at my heels –

what do you want,
what do you want?

I want a good lover
who will keep her mouth shut
except for my praise to my face
or loudly behind my back;
who hates my enemies
and willingly suffers indignities –

what do you want?

I want a lover
who suffers indignities.

PUBLIC LIBRARY

So I sat day after day in the smoking room of the library
some book or paper or magazine on my knee
smoking   half reading
half in a dreamed trance   half listening
to the sounds around me   half looking
at the people around me

the sounds   shuffling of canvas covered feet
rubber soled feet   moccasined feet
newspapers being borrowed   being shaken
rustling like a sea or wind
sea of other peoples' lives
wind a movement of other peoples' air and breathing
books crackling as their backs were broken
the flick/flick of fingertips
and fingernails on the corners of pages
snap of shutting decisively
or accidentally   plump lackadaisically
muted thump of being tossed on low tables
abandoned as too boring
having small type and big ideas or big type and small ideas
magazines slapping against other magazines
heavy glossy pages scraping and sliding against each other
pieces of paper being torn   irritating noise
magnification of a snail's death scream
being stepped on   and the sounds of the people

snores grunts slobbers   sighs
aimless and tuneless humming
toneless and breathless whispering of unknown tunes
noise of the man who sat all day
from nine-thirty in the morning until nine at night
going aaah aaah   every four seconds
the man who blew his nose noisily between his fingertips
ten times an hour
and snapped the slime off his hand   slap
the asthmatic breathing of another
the man who talked to himself
in a strange sounding language
something slavic or made up
giggling and twittering between the phrases
his laughter rising as the day went on
to a higher and higher more hysterical pitch
until when it seemed he would finally have to collapse
from giggling he suddenly flushed
as if insulted by himself
and screamed in english   the anguish language
Son of a bitch   son of a bitch you
put on his hat and left to go home and make supper
for himself in some grey room

old men snorting in bewildered hurt derision at the newspapers
and trying to suck up the mucus in their noses
without having to show a dirty handkerchief
so strong their pride
feeling passed by   abandoned
left alone by all the other billions

matches being drawn along plaster walls
scraping like magazine pages
small explosions of wooden matches
cigarettes lustily sucked on
cigarettes thrown on the floor
cigarettes ground out with hate on the floor
revenge against old men's diseases
cancer possibilities   against the all night
long coughing and spitting themselves
and the neighbours' coughing and spitting also

people   in canvas shoes   rubber soles
loggers' boots   years-old oxfords with great cavities
moccasins   thick grey woolen socks knee high
old army issue from two wars at least
baggy cuffless pants   cotton workshirts
flannel plaids sweated in for twenty summers and winters
brassbound army and police suspenders
mismatched doublebreasted fantastically wide lapelled
old pointed blue pinstripe suitcoats
relics of other generations   the wearers outside
all generations   other excitements   dancing
polkas in the northland or on the prairies
to screechy violins and accordions
heavy brown horsey overcoats pulling down their thin shoulders
white beard stubble with tobacco stains
grey beard stubble   white hair
grey hair   trembly hands   rheumy eyes
pale watery eyes   shallow ponds
huge bulging veins popping out from necks and foreheads
glasses with cracked lenses

only here and there the younger ones within twenty years of me
a little neater   the hair still coloured
dull the veins
and breathing and spit a little less obvious
a hint of combs and razor blades
and rarely the well-dressed
tightly-girdle-assed pointy-wire-breasted and well-stroked
young woman would come in and look about
as if she had blundered into the wrong toilet
afraid to walk out again immediately
lest we be too obviously insulted

choosing a chair   trying to look unconcerned
lighting a cigarette   sitting in her stiff brassiere
with all the men who could see far enough staring furtively
at her fat knees   shifting around in their chairs
to ease the strain on the crotches of their greasy pants
as forgotten juices stirred

– when her cigarette was half smoked the woman
girl that is   would butt it in the ashtray   fold
her book   carefully preserving the place
and leave for a safer floor on the building
one where she would not feel those shifty eyes
on her breasts   eyes on her legs
evil male eyes endeavouring to see up her
tight skirts   to see her sweating thighs
to see

and sometimes heavy businessmen
come in and blunder out again
like cardiac bears
but of them
I will not speak for I do not know.

NO SONG

said the bird
in its attitude

caw

declining
the privilege
of music
or melody

caw

standing
on its tree

caw

fingering
the absolute
wood
beneath

LIKE A CANADIAN

What does a person want
out of life: images?

Don't try to drive me
crazy. A civil service pension

and an odd legation
is good enough for me. Nah.

Bugger the prairies
and their crazy trees,

bugger the patriots
and their knock-knees,

I'm starting to feel sentimental
only when at home

in my sixty-dollar-a-month slum,
or to feel like a Canadian

only when kissing someone else's bum.
It's a hard life. Them damn trees

keep on pretending I'm not here. Tough.
But not as tough as living with the Crees.

THE SQUIRREL PEANUT-BUTTER SONG

Time to do something
like taking a nap
or a knapsack and going
to Saskatoon or Montreal
or getting drunk
or getting married

At times I find life
difficult to understand
but only rarely

It is then that I stop
making a fool of myself
but only rarely

Why for instance
does a friend send me
a can containing fifty Japanese
cigarettes called Peace

There is a stylized drawing
of a dove on the can
a dove falling on its head

I nearly went crazy with rage
trying to open the can

Or why do the rich
sometimes think it is virtuous
to be poor and why do the poor
think it is virtuous to be poor
answer: they don't

And why do I keep a dried flower
brown-orange
wired to the carrier bar
of my dusty typewriter
answer: I am too lazy to take it off

Why do I have fifty pencils
of various colours including gold
and four ink pens
and a dozen ballpoints at least
when writing by hand gives me cramps

I must be out of shape
a simple wooden matchstick
dipped in my blood would be sufficient
for signing my name to begging letters

Why isn't there a deep reason for everything
or why can't I be serious
I want to have a decent excuse for getting drunk
like a tragic childhood or adulthood
or unbearable secrets and incurable diseases
that would be better than just liking it

And why go to Montreal
I am no good with languages
an admission
I didn't do it to learn French
I did it so I could come back
and say I have just been to Montreal
picking dew-worms is a terrible job
I had better get married
fast

SOLITAIRE

Then he ran away,
the forest going by him

like a motion picture
and the road slid

beneath his feet
until he stumbled in a ditch

beside a small meadow,
hardly a lawn,

with stiff green grass
tough as barb wire,

around an abandoned
plank shack inhabited

by rats, near a shallow
rocky river in the north

of nowhere, and stayed there
with nightmare

and pack rats and water
and wet chocolate bars and cigarettes

until an engine came
and took him back again.

THE MIRROR

In the night of toothpaste and Indian songs,
lockjaw and cigarettes, stewed tomatoes,
the patterns swinging children make, the patterns
made by jets over the mountains, officially approved,
the stars, cars, clouds of fog, cloudy water, cold sand,
in a note of December, lights, wars, water flooding water,
faith, love, hope –

This is not a new poem,
it is an old poem I am writing for the first time
today, of water and the wars, love, time, flesh
flooding the universe with dying sounds,
all the languages of death the same, in tubes,
instruments, rooms, blocks, cities, promontories,
provinces, countries, even my dearest
Canada, continents, earth and our planets, the world
of cigarette butts spinning about the sun to quickening gunfire –

Of the son's pledge fighting in Asia,
men punishing environment, pitted
against a vastly greater involvement
in the waning monsoon mud months, disheartened
the men and divided the Pacific lake, incredible.

Now that all things are moving
'beyond the age of enmity,' what will you do? –
admiring in the silver chemical mirror yourself,
civil, western, gentle, spiteful, man
brushing the dogs like corpulent lice
from off your back.

SAMUEL HEARNE IN WINTERTIME

1. In this cold room
I remember the smell of manure
on men's heavy clothes as good,
the smell of horses.

It is a romantic world
to readers of journeys
to the Northern Ocean –

especially if their houses are heated
to some degree, Samuel.

Hearne, your camp must have smelled
like hell whenever you settled down
for a few days of rest and journal-work:

hell smeared with human manure,
hell half-full of raw hides,
hell of sweat, Indians, stale fat,
meat-hell, fear-hell, hell of cold.

2. One child is back from the doctor's while
the other one wanders about in dirty pants
and I think of Samuel Hearne and the land –

puffy children coughing as I think,
crying, sick-faced,
vomit stirring in grey blankets
from room to room.

It is Christmastime
the cold flesh shines.
No praise in merely enduring.

3. Samuel Hearne did more
in the land (like all the rest

full of rocks and hilly country,
many very extensive tracts of land,
tittimeg, pike and barble,

and the islands:
the islands, many
of them abound

as well as the main
land does
with dwarf woods,

chiefly pine
in some parts intermixed
with larch and birch) than endure.

The Indians killed twelve deer.
It was impossible to describe
the intenseness of the cold.

4. And, Samuel Hearne,
I have almost begun to talk

as if you wanted to be
gallant, as if you went
through that land for a book –

as if you were not SAM, wanting
to know, to do a job.

5. There was that Eskimo girl
at Bloody Fall, at your feet,

Samuel Hearne, with two spears in her,
you helpless before your helpers,

and she twisted about them like
an eel, dying, never to know

THE BIG BEND

1. It goes on in
the past and
the mystery,

steel rusts in
the river,
the cautioning

signs are down,
there will be
incidents

as even the
attempt fades,
the imperfect

mood denoting
an action, all
men are able

to own,
not yet completed.

2. Apply the principle
of time to
discover

the fault fades out, the mice
run free, the
wild woman

of the woods
(d'sonoqua)
leaves, rats

inhabit the shacks
of dead men.

3. We are the masters
of the dead
shale on the roadway,

masters of
that, but
also part

of the embryo,
shadows and
red light:

palingenesia,
the qualitative change
furiously

hanging
over a flowering bush.

4. The bridges break,
liquid
seeps through the ground,

what is
invented?

5. Go without
vanity now, momentum
more definite:

water splashes
the rocks, how
to define

an imperfect flower,
no silence in
the forest   who knows

what he remembers
or what he invented?

6. Time may be counted,
permutating
series of

disintegrations
used against
each other, ours

and the roadway's (the
same thing), sepals,
petal, stamens, pistils,

the same
watery forest, broken
bridges, the same unequal

series of
equal units of
discovery:

you, North America,
remote
in the night,

among the trees
and flowers
from anther
to stigma

unused.

THE PRIDE

1. The image/ the pawnees
in their earth-lodge villages,
the clear image
of teton sioux, wild
fickle people the chronicler says,

the crazy dogs, men
tethered with leather dog-thongs
to a stake, fighting until dead,

image: arikaras
with traded spanish sabre blades
mounted on the long
heavy buffalo lances,
riding the sioux
down, the centaurs, the horsemen
scouring the level plains
in war or hunt
until smallpox got them,
the warriors,

image – of a desolate country,
a long way between fires,
unfound lakes, mirages, cold rocks,
and lone men going through it,
cree with good guns
causing terror in athabaska
among the inhabitants, frightened
stone-age people, 'so that
they fled at the mere sight
of a strange smoke miles away.'

2. This western country crammed
with the ghosts of indians,
haunting the coastal stones and shores,
the forested pacific islands,
mountains, hills and plains:

beside the ocean ethlinga,
man in the moon, empties
his bucket, on
a sign from spirit
of the wind ethlinga
empties his bucket, refreshing
the earth, and it rains
on the white cities;

that black joker, broken-
jawed raven, most prominent
among haida and tsimshian tribes
is in the kwakiutl
dance masks too –
it was he who brought fire,
food and water to man,
the trickster;

and thunderbird hilunga,
little thought of
by haida for lack of thunderstorms
in their district, goes
by many names, exquisite disguises
carved in the painted wood,

he is nootka tootooch, the wings
causing thunder and the tongue
or flashing eyes engendering
rabid white lightning,
whose food was whales,

called kwunusela by the kwakiutl,
it was he who laid down the house-logs
for the people at the place
where kwunusela alighted;

in full force and virtue
and terror of the law, eagle –
he is authority, the sun
assumed his form once,
the sun which used to be
a flicker's egg, success-
fully transformed;

and malevolence comes to the land,
the wild woman of the woods –
grinning, she wears
a hummingbird in her hair,
d'sonoqua, the furious one –

they are all ready
to be found, the legends
and the people, or
all their ghosts and memories,
whatever is strong enough
to be remembered.

3. But what image, bewildered
son of all men
under the hot sun,
do you worship,
what completeness
do you hope to have
from these tales,
a half-understood massiveness, mirage,
in men's minds – what
is your purpose;

with what force
will you proceed
along a line
neither straight nor short,
whose future
you cannot know
or result foretell,
whose meaning is still
obscured as the incidents
occur and accumulate?

4. The country moves on;
there are orchards in the interior,
the mountain passes
are broken, the foothills
covered with cattle and fences,
and the fading hills covered;

but the plains are bare,
not barren, easy
for me to love their people,
for me to love their people
without selection.

5. In 1787, the old cree saukamappee, aged 75 or thereabout, speaking then of things that had happened when he was 16, just a man, told david thompson about the raids the shoshonis, the snakes, had made on the westward-reaching peigan, of their war-parties sometimes sent 10 day's journey to enemy camps, the men all afoot in battle array for the encounter, crouching behind their giant shields. The peigan armed with guns drove these snakes out of the plains, the plains where their strength had been, where they had been settled since living memory (though nothing is remembered beyond a grandfather's time), to the west of the rockies:

these people moved without rest,
backward and forward with the wind,
the seasons, the game, great herds,
in hunger and abundance –

in summer and in the bloody fall
they gathered on the killing grounds,
fat and shining with fat, amused
with the luxuries of war and death,

relieved from the steam of knowledge,
consoled by the stream of blood
and steam rising from the fresh hides
and tired horses, wheeling in their pride
on the sweating horses, their pride.

6. Those are all stories;
the pride, the grand poem
of our land, of the earth itself,
will come, welcome, and
sought for, and found,
in a line of running verse,
sweating, our pride;

we seize on
what has happened before,
one line only
will be enough,
a single line
and then the sunlit brilliant image suddenly floods us
with understanding, shocks our
attentions, and all desire
stops, stands alone;

we stand alone,
we are no longer lonely
but have roots,
and the rooted words
recur in the mind, mirror, so that
we dwell on nothing else, in nothing else,
touched, repeating them,
at home freely
at last, in amazement;

'the unyielding phrase
in tune with the epoch,'
the thing made up
of our desires,
not of its words, not only
of them, but of something else
as well, that which we desire
so ardently, that which
will not come when
it is summoned alone,
but grows in us
and idles about and hides
until the moment is due –

the knowledge of
our origins, and where
we are in truth,
whose land this is
and is to be.

7. The unyielding phrase:
when the moment is due, then
it springs upon us
out of our own mouths,
unconsidered, overwhelming
in its knowledge, complete –

not this handful
of fragments, as the indians
are not composed of
the romantic stories
about them, or of the stories
they tell only, but
still ride the soil
in us, dry bones a part
of the dust in our eyes,
needed and troubling
in the glare, in
our breath, in our
ears, in our mouths,
in our bodies entire, in our minds, until
at last
we become them

in our desires, our desires,
mirages, mirrors, that are theirs, hard-
riding desires, and they
become our true forbears, moulded
by the same wind or rain,
and in this land we
are their people, come
back to life again.

From THE CAVE, 1970

THE FLOWER

I am too tense,
decline to dance
verbally. The flower
is not in its colour,
but in the seed.

THE ENGINE AND THE SEA

The locomotive in the city's distance, obscure, misplaced,
sounds a child's horn on the flat land leading to the
cliff of dark buildings,

the foghorns on the water's edge cry back.

Between the sounds men sit in their houses watching
machines inform them in Edison's light. In the marshes,
the music of ominous living...

a leggy insect runs on that surface, frogs wait, fish,
angling birds.

In the cities men wait to be told. They sit between the
locomotive and the fish. The flat sea and the prairie that
was a sea contain them. Images float before their eyes,

men and women acting,

entertaining, rigorously dancing with fractured minds
contorted to a joyless pleasure, time sold from life.

The locomotive hums, the prairies hum. Frogs touch
insects with their long tongues, the cannibal fish and the
stabbing birds

wait.

Night actions flash before uncountable animal eyes. Mice
run. Light rain falls in the night.

The frogs are stilled. Between the engine and the sea, the
lights go out. People sleep with mechanical dreams, the sea
hums with rain, the locomotive shines black, fish wait under
the surface of a pinked pool.

Frogs shiver in the cold. The land waits, black, dreaming.
Men lie dry in their beds.

History, history!

Under the closed lids their eyes flick back and forth as
they try to follow the frightening shapes of their desires.

WARM WIND

The wet sun shines a muddy spring,
warm wind blows; I walk, content
with the weather of our hands.

What if the world does not end,
and we are only stained shadows
the sidewalk photographed? Today

I hold you and have a happiness
that makes me human once again.

THE WIND

On this last desperate day
when the enchanting devil and the formless hero
embrace, when the wind in our minds
is a maniac, when our flesh is slack
as plastic, melted with desire,

let us see each other entire
and exhausted by each other, turning
about and about to escape,
as we have these months – then leave,
dreaming what we might have been.

DOUKHOBOR

When you die and your weathery corpse
lies on the chipped kitchen table,

the wind blowing the wood of your house
painted in shades of blue, farmer

out from Russia as the century turned,
died, and lay at the feet of the wars,

who will ever be able to say for you
what you thought at the sight of the Czar's horsemen

riding with whips among you, the sight
of the rifles burning on bonfires,

the long sea-voyage, strange customs endured,
officials changing your name

into the strange script that covered the stores,
the polite brown men who spoke no language

you understood and helped you
free your team from Saskatchewan winter mud,

who will be able to say for you
just what you thought as the villages marched

naked to Eden and the English
went to war and came back again

with their funny ways, proud
to speak of killing each other, you, whose mind

refused to slaughter, refused the blood,
you who will lie in your house, stiff as winter,

dumb as an ox, unable to love,
while your women sob and offer the visitors tea?

THE PRAIRIE

One compiles, piles, plies
these masses of words, verbs,
massifs, mastiffs barking meaning,
dried chips
of buffalo dung, excreta from beasts

the prairie fed, foddered,
food for generations: men roaming
as beasts seen through dips
in history, fostered by legend,
invented remembrance. Scenes shake,

the words do not suffice. One bred
on the same earth wishes himself
something different, the other's
twin, impossible thing, twining
both memories, a double meaning,

but cannot be – never
to be at ease, but always migrating
from city to city
seeking some almost seen
god or food or earth or word.

BEFORE SLEEP

Until you lie down in the dark again
to see with nightmare this depressed slant
of winter light   a cold sick yellow
clouded   morose   that lies on your eyes

before you sleep   ideas locked
firmly in place   before you sleep
to wake and wash the sleep from your face

with cold water   cupped in your hands
that have curled in nightmare
half the night long   until the fear
clings to the back of your mind   only forgotten

until you lie down in the dark again to see
the white faces floating and the mouths that say
urgently   Listen to me   Listen only to me

the familiar faces like fathers turning
just out of sight of the dreaming eyes   names
almost remembered   mothers of hatred and fear
and cousins to murder   strangers seeking

you for themselves   Remember how real
your waking life seemed   until you lay down
in the dark and pulled
a sheet to your head

REVENGE

He thought of the hammer.
He got up, holding his arm
as if it were already broken.

He went downstairs again.
Coming into the kitchen
he held up his arm before his eyes,

gloating, already triumphant.
They'll feel sorry for me,
they'll feel sorry for me.

He let go of the arm, got
a plain glass out of the cupboard,
filled it with cold tapwater.

He drank, he regarded his arm,
he considered the hammer.
Exultation strengthened in him.

BY THE GREY ATLANTIC

Among the green trees of Vancouver
it was being in a dream,
a dream of life, remembered,
the future recalled; dream men,
dream women, walking.

Here by the grey Atlantic
it is being a dream
of death remembered,
the past recalled; dead men
and dead women, talking.

GOD BLESS YOU

What I like is this Atlantic.
Guns practise outside my window.

But, this ocean: here men have drowned.
You can see it in the grey waves.

Eyes roll in the troughs, hands reach.
White flesh drapes the actual weeds.

This is water men die, not swim, in.
God bless you, if you go in a bathing suit

to hell.

REMEMBERING CHRISTOPHER SMART

Being a small person bound
in a small circle, I think
of large things, obscurely....

But what is so obscure
as I am, my brothers? I can discern
the motives that impel me,
not fight them. Wearing clothes
annoys me but every morning
I get up and pull my underwear on.

When I think of my cat Boots,
grey as dawn but white-legged,
who took over the whole chesterfield
from my fat father who'd won a military medal
in the first world war,
and lay there insolently stretched out,
the whole body yawning as cats do,
I see that even amoebas can rule the world,
and who says the justice would be less?

No. When I consider a small person
such as myself, dreaming of women,
those legs once again and that warmness,
just to lie there, to lie,
I see that we all make the world what we want.
Our disappointment lies in the world as it is.

AMERICA

Even the dissident ones speak
as members of an Empire, residents
of the centre of the earth. Power
extends from their words
to all the continents and their modesty
is liable for millions. How must it be
to be caught in the Empire, to have
everything you do matter? Even
treason is imperial; the scornful
self-abuse comes from inside the boundaries
of the possible. Outside the borders of royalty
the barbarians wait in fear,
finding it hard to know which prince
to believe; trade-goods comfort them,
gadgets of little worth, cars, television,
refrigerators, for which they give iron,
copper, uranium, gold, trees, and water,
worth of all sorts for the things
citizens of Empire take as their due.

In the Empire power speaks from the poorest
and culture flourishes. Outside the boundaries
the barbarians imitate styles and send their sons,
the talented hirelings, to learn and to stay;
the sons of their sons will be princes too,
in the Estate where even the unhappy
carry an aura of worldly power; and the lords
of power send out directives
for the rest of the world to obey. If they live
in the Empire, it matters what they say.

ALCAZAR

I think I've seen you somewhere,
said the girl in the pub, sitting
at the next table. We joined her,
but could not think where
we might have been together.

At the same table, the fat woman
(happy or sad) said, I wish
I was a bird, I'd take my suitcase
in my beak and fly away
to Copenhagen. Copenhagen?

But that girl in the pub: she was plump,
not smart. She sat
with her husband, married
after a 9-day knowledge of him,
English sailor, ship-jumper.

I'm flying to Copenhagen,
the fat woman said; her suitcase
was not in her beak. The girl and I
could not think where we might have been
together. The beer mounted in us.

The fat woman dreamed. The sailor
complained of the beer and the cigarettes here;
the girl spoke of her marriage
and husband. It would be all right, she said,
if he wouldn't burn me with cigarettes.

HOW THE WEATHER IS

In Deep Cove they reported rain.
In the District of Coquitlam

the rain has started. In Burnaby
the snow is mixed with rain. But here

there is only snow
and influenza, wet coughing

from room to room in the winter.
I am winning

large imaginary sums of money
at solitaire, shouting:

That's enough, kids!
I want to have a good time.

Or to be good, after
being a fool.

Mixed rain and snow, slush
is out East Hastings way now,

moving closer as the weather
breaks, exchanging

one discomfort for another –
less so. The children

are giggling on a chair together
between fights. What

can it be? We're having
fun daddy just

playing games they say, surrounded
by the world.

THE APPARITION

An apparition slackwitted
    with disaster climbed
into the bus today,
    red hair, hunchbacked,
Richard the Third's movie face,
    thin white propped legs,
a brown coat, speckled
    white and brown dishcover
hat, flat, something
    to enfold a dish of cold potatoes –

her discontent
    hangs in the air,
a thick curdled yellow floating
    in the dissatisfied air
as she has a friendly
    little talk with the driver,
pout wrinkling the long chin,
    handsome face obscurely handsome,
very definite, set,
    set in eccentricity, uncalculated
finally, finally necessary,
    an abandoned pasture –

posture (the mind's stutter
    as it avoids what has happened
and tries to invent concern
    beyond what is important) –

life made mad by metabolism
    of the shoulder-blades and legs,
no distortion innate
    in the mind but that forced on it
by the world and the unslavelike body.

THE FAT MAN

1. A fat man holding flowers regards the traffic light
above him, hand made fist around
the flowers and the paper that wraps their stems, hand
balancing on the abrupt ridge of his stomach,
a shelf. The hand, furthest forward in space,
followed then by his face placed back
even more, necklessly leaning on the sloping shoulders
above a spindle-chest:
this hand makes a straight line passing
through the blooms of the flowers,
through the fat man's open black mouth, by the back of his head
to the glass light of the traffic signal.

He regards the glare of the signal, the light it gives, not
the thing itself. Light from it
slants down his forehead, bounces over the eyebrows'
projecting spur of bone, leaving the sockets themselves
dark. He is a fat and male Orphan Annie
with black eyes. Light divides along his nose and dribbles
off his chin. Led down that trail, it scatters
amongst the petals of the flowers and then
diffuses in diluted patches on his hand.

Light rain begins to fall. A small wind drives.
At night the ocean wind this time of year
brings rain. I turn my face and let
the little water sting me. The fat man
has not moved. He still observes
the traffic-signal's glow. He will not let it
get away.
He moves his hat
over the flowers, a gesture. Water
spatters off his half-bald head. A gesture;
he does not need to do that. The flowers do not
need protection from the rain; he does.
He has no petals; he is more than half-bald.

Oh, hair covers half his skull
but that hair is thin; it streams
about his ears. His hair is cut
long at the sides: pretence of hairiness;
he suspects that the office boys call him
skinhead or bonehead, as he would have done
if things were different or reversed.

2. Perhaps the girls
call him bonehead too,
behind his back
or around corners,
out of the sides
of their lovely mouths;
he was almost sure
that he might have heard
one of those girls
saying bonehead about him
to another, the big one,
the big girl saying.

He is taking the flowers
home to his wife
but now his hair
is wet and it hangs
down like a dog's,
obeying the rain
and the slanting wind;
he holds his head back
to catch the light,
he does not want
to lose a second; he
has paid for time.

The rain makes even me
sniff and as for him
it is now running down

both sides of his nose
in the red light.
The raindrops spatter
on the top of his head,
microcosmic atomics.
He does not uncover
the flowers, the brim
of his hat still covers
the grasping hand. His arm
ends at the shirtcuff.
The hand is obscured.

If he does that enough
it will make him sick.
He is bald and fat and aging
and that is enough.
He will catch pneumonia
or even TB,
and at the office they
will say that that was right
because he is a tuber,
a sweet potato. He knows
the jokes they make.

And he would die
from tuberculosis
or even if he survived
he would lie for years
in a white sanatorium,
antiseptic, and cough
phlegm spotted with blood
and spit phlegm spotted
with red red blood
into his handkerchief
or into some old
wadded-up bits
of toilet paper.
He would have to keep

a roll on the table
beside his bed;
there could never be
handkerchiefs enough
and everyone would see
the handy toilet paper
and know what it was for,
and on the white enamelled
table there would be
a water glass with two or three
small flowers in it.
He would grow sick of their look
and smell. He hates flowers.

The nurse would put new blooms
into the glass each week
and there would be brown stains
around the middle of the glass
as the dirty water she forgot
evaporated. And the pretty nurse
would watch him spitting phlegm
spotted with red red blood
into his little piece
of wadded-up toilet paper and she
would feel disgusted –
how much easier life would be
if only women were ugly!

But perhaps he will just catch a cold.
Nothing has happened yet.
Even the worst of dreams
sometimes fails to come true.
At least he will catch a cold;
it will make him miserable
all winter and he
will have to wipe his nose
in the middle of composing letters

into the dictaphone, or blow.
He will be forced to sniff
during the prayers in church,
as if he disapproved.

3. He should let the rain fall on the flowers equally
with his head so that they will last long enough
to ornament his coffin when he dies. Red flowers
will ornament his coffin when he dies
while his wife and the mourners twirl round him.

The office boys and the girls from the office
will stand stiff in the pews to watch
the coffin covered with red light thrown
from the stained glass of the church,
windows showing the martyrdoms of saints.

They will not see his face because his head
will be turned to the altar, his feet
turned toward them; his stomach will be in the way.
Perhaps the people in charge or his wife
will forget to buy him new shoes for the service.

His feet will be wearing his best
pair of black shoes, worn on the bottoms:
but they will all forget he was bald,
he will have flowers instead of hair,
and no one will ever again see his face.

4. No, they won't forget.
Salesmen will come into the office
and ask if so-and-so is in,
his own dead name. The secretaries will say,
Dead Name? I don't remember him....
Oh yes, the bald one, he isn't here anymore,
I think he left or something....

5. The traffic light turned green.
It cast its night-time vegetative glow
onto the fat man's raised face, changing it
into a puffed-up lime. He brought
down his head. He was dead already.
Green light glinted off the whites of his eyes,
exposed now. His mouth closed.
Bald man. Fat man. He stepped off the edge
of the sidewalk as off
the roof of the world's tallest building.
Darkness and rain gathered about him
as he walked down the tunnelling street,
a tarpaper blob retreating with flowers, home
to sleep and dreams and his apple-pie wife.

THE CAVE

The stars are your deathbed.
You rest from the cave
to Pluto or whatever dark planets
lie beyond. No ideas trap you.

In the unobstructed sunlight miles high
the Earth is beautiful as a postcard.
Sinai looks as the map says it should,
and people are too small to be observed.

In Africa there are no trees to see.
It is a map world.
The sunlight is brilliant
as a two-carat diamond on a girl's hand.

The girl is young, visible to your mind,
growing older. Beyond Pluto
and the darkest planets, children surround her.

The diamond glows on her finger
like a worm. The stars, the stars
shine like one-carat diamonds. Beyond
Pluto and the darkest planets the stars shine.

The diamonds shine in wormy rings
on fingers, in coffins of unobstructed space.
The flesh circles the bone in strips
in the coffin as the ring circled flesh.

The two-carat sun hangs loosely,
just restraining the Earth. Beyond the planets,
beyond the dark coffin, beyond the ring of stars,
your bed is in the shining, tree-lit cave.

From LIES, 1972

AND THE DEAD ROSE UP FROM THE WATER

Coming alive at the age of thirty,
refusing a few years
to abandon my despair,
and the dead rose up from the water,
their heads buoys in front of my love;
I tried to kiss them alone
but the water moved their pale fleshy faces.

This year ten million Bengalis
met old enemies – exile
and cholera, bullets, knives. This year
corpses returned from the moon. Traitors
to humans flourished.

Children…children, what are you doing?
I despair of *you.*
I don't care if you kill yourselves, but
why kill me? I have only come alive
for a moment; and I wish I were dead,
or kissing the ocean's lovers,
brown foam on their opened eyes.

EVERY MUDDY ROAD

Every muddy road I walk along
I am the man who knows all about Jesus
but doesn't believe. My fat ass
trudges on. I am so weary. Lord;
beer is my muse, my music. And you –
if you could see this country,
you would weep too. Who wants love,
on any muddy road he walks along?

You know that every time I try to slip
you hold me up. And when I wish
the cars would kill me they drive on by;
they have some place to go,
someone to meet, a chance,
some other death to die, not a muddy bleeding.

You know that every muddy word I write
cries. You know that I have slipped,
but not to die. You know
that in this mud no one cares
for tears but you. You would have loved yourself
if others had.

THE HERO AROUND ME

Water submissive and cool, the abundant sun
hot on my white back, day
of quiet pleasures, air humming
a steady soothing tune through the long hours,
ghosts slowly drifting past,
heads like broad arrows, hair coiled
about faces. Time is sliding away....

I have desired many
but I wonder if I have loved one? –
remembering the cruel amusement and pleasure
of a youth called hard-hearted,
joy in a tearful eye and a frantic manner,
dismissive joy, and the day
humming and sliding away....

Once heroes marched through my mind
in solid ranks, the deeds
shaped pointedly, and I knew
I could never be one of them,
though I desired it, wished for one sharp moment
in my life – thinking
of the hero as man in combat only....

The day came, but not as war.
Fields of grain around me were crystal,
the sky polished, endless gold and blue,
and in the still heat a meadowlark
twisted its sculptured tune around me
once, quickly, a deft feat of superior magic,
and all time stopped, world without end,
and I was as a tree is, loathing nothing.

THE SKY

Never knowing how we got there
one day we woke and saw the sky,
limitless, serene, capable
of black cloud and lightning,
the land limitless, yellow
with grain in summertime,
light green in spring, stretching
to the edge of the world
but never ending; and it made us
want to go.
                                We travelled westward,
a little further every time,
venturing the hills, venturing
the spirit-inhabited mountains,
the quick down-slope, viewing at last
the sea and the sea-city.

The city was wonderful, huge;
we never heard that there were no birds.

How small all our own cities seemed,
so tiny, one street only, limited,
lacking the towers, the veritable ocean,
strange trees.
                                Later we woke,
and saw the sky, crammed by mountains
as we were, open only to the sea,
westward; and could not swim.

MY DREAMS

There's a strange dog
puking in my sink
where I wash the dishes.
I wish I were blind.

My dreams speak to me
in faint phony English accents;
the zippers of my dreams
are frozen solid.

I only looked outside
and my ears went ping;
my dreams walked a thousand miles
in search of mountains.

What they found
was Calgary; they tried to climb
a hotel
with old-fashioned equipment.

Now there are needles
in the ears of my dreams.
There is frost on their eyes.
They try to be brave about shovels.

My dreams fell off everything they tried.
They lie flat on their backs
pointing newcomers in the wrong direction.

WHITE LIES

The winter shines, I think.
But it's summer now and I'm not home.
The sky is the colour of a pike's belly,
the air stinks. It is pretending
to be about to rain. The atmosphere
is heavy, is glue. Glum glue.

I seem to remember those winters.
The hard-surfaced snow
would have stretched tightly
over the low hills, vast pearls
glowing in the night of five o'clock,
white lies.

Bright cars cautious on the roads,
the grey skeleton trees, occasional greens,
rarely a rabbit's convulsive flash,
black birds sitting on telephone wires,
waiting, waiting.

I haven't been home for years.

SLOW SPRING

Lime-green pants and a red polka-dot handkerchief,
  hanging-on-a-line.
  The trees are sallow, trying
    to pretend to be alive. Touch them
And your fingers
Will stick together
  like people on a slow train.
  Their eyes follow you everywhere, yellow and grey.

The air is colder than your dreams could be.
The carved boulder in your shoe
  is only a pebble,
    and small.
In the wind spider webs sway.
This is Spring, soft ashes falling to the ground.

COMPANY

1. It is a man.

   It sits in the public library
   coveting the women it fears.

   They sense it has been without a woman a long time
   and they loathe it.

   They smell the worst kind of celibacy on it,
   involuntary.

   There is a rancidness, a smell of having given up,
   of having been given up on:
   if no one cares then no one will care.

   It is not the worn jeans
   or the shirt seeming to have been on one day too long
   no matter how newly washed;
   it is not the fingernails, cut or uncut, dirty or clean,
   or the yellow tobacco smear along the side of the finger,
   or the hair, combed or uncombed;
   it is not a matter of fixing the teeth,
   nothing to do with blackheads
   or with the awkward shape or even with money:
   women are generous when they are able to be.

   It is the smell of hopelessness,
   it is fear's emanation, that ulcerates the stomach.
   Women edge away from it, feeling something unhuman,
   the wrong condition of longing, the wrong character of need,
   the long time waiting.

2. It loves company and company is disgusted by it;
company enjoys being disgusted by it;
it enjoys disgusting company.

It thinks that it likes to act
as company expects it to act:
cadging, begging, groping,
insolent subservience,
arrogant whining.

In the nape of its neck it feels
that it knows all about people,
what they think or expect:
but they know all about it. They are willing
to enjoy their disgust, to be amused,
so long as the price is not too high.
When the price is too high
they will cease to be amused.

Then it will not have company.
It will have to go somewhere else.

The same things will occur in another place.
Things will always occur.
And back again. The same rhythms.
But shorter
durations. The time
always gets shorter. Until
in a rush at last there is no time.
At all.

3. It will sit sour in seventy-five-cent
or free Salvation Army and welfare barracks
and tell the other bums what it might have been
or done
and listen to what they might have been or done –
moving from cot to cot,
and all of the beds in all of the cities the same.

4. Sky blue.
Phony-looking fluffy white postcard clouds
lumping slowly along in the hot sky.

Beach with grass, washed-up logs, sand.
Then mixed sand and shells and pebbles,
and dark green-black vegetable sludge from the sea.

Then pebbles and sludge and shells,
then stones and shells,
then yellowish foam flecked with white,
then small fat lazy rolls of water
with sticks floating on it.

Fuelling stations for boats anchored in the water,
a few power boats, a few sail boats,
the ocean.

And impossible miles across there are the islands of the Pacific,
imagined decorations in a romantic atlas, alien histories,
Polynesia, Melanesia, Micronesia…an atlas
full of life –

Even if the cannibals dance,
anywhere but here where people know it….

5. It doubles over,
takes off its shoes and socks.

It sits down on the sand,
hands propped behind it,
legs stuck stiffly out;
it feels a trace of shame.

It is pale.
There is dirt between its toes and around the nails.
It digs its feet into the sand to cover them.

The sun is hot.
Gulls squawk.

There are girls and women on the beach and in the water.
It tries not to look at the flesh.

6. Memories drift past;
they cannot be grasped.

To remember without lying is difficult.
With friends, drinking beer, there is a set of rules,
a code of telling –
                                        that covers the errors,
the cowardices and stupidities,
turning them into weak amusing virtues,
anecdotes in which no one really wins or loses.

7. When there are no friends
at least there must be companions occasionally.

It would be too much
to sit in a room alone all of the time
or on the edge of a cot in a noisy room.

8. Remembering seems like a slow train now,
that goes on its tracks.

To ride is to go where the train goes,
or the way the train goes,
though not always all the way.

Not always?
Never.

9. It takes its feet out of the sand.
It stands up and walks to the edge of the ocean.

Wavelets cover its feet and touch its ankles at times.
The water is cool and pleasant.

It walks back to where it had been
and stands looking at its feet.

It has forgotten the girls and women on the beach,
the flesh.
When its feet are dry it will put on its socks and shoes
and walk off the beach
with its head down
and cross the bridge to the centre of the city
to the smoking room of the public library.

10. Perhaps something will happen.
Perhaps something good will happen.

Perhaps it will meet someone it knows
or someone who knows it.

Him.

They would talk together about the past.
They would agree with each other.
They would drink beer and smoke and talk confidently
about women
until closing time.

Then they would part,
not contradicting each other.

CROW WALKING

I don't think he ever saw that crow
drinking in the sun as though it knew
what the moon was all about,
I don't think he ever found
that there was anyone else but him;
there was something, but not a birth
of heroic futures.

No prime ministers phoned. The football games
didn't turn out the way he planned; halfbacks
slid in the mud as they made their cuts. Help him,
when the player falls down so neatly;
help him when the band plays a foreign anthem,
when the papers arrive on time, poor words:
they are not the colour of the sky.

Life continued before it occurred.
Out in the kitchen where the hamburger fried
Jesus was hiding among the wieners. Life
went on, went on, poems interrupted by toast,
the green mountains swaying, the still sea of snow,
the beds of the weathered houses, there was something.
He tried to remember.

At last he saw the crow walking, dipping its head.
He saw the strands of filament shining;
he dreamed of the irreclaimable sea
and went to an office, machines,
he turned to the law, the law, the law,
and dreams of appreciative women pacing in feathers,
merit allowing applause.

Man, change your accent, get rid
of that hunky name! Teach yourself to speak,
not spit. If you must die,
do it alone. And if you must remember,
recall that you will never walk
this way again. Your trees are green and gone:
do you see that crow? Kill it.

GROSS MASKS

No world without demons, no island
not surrounded by sharks.

Gross masks in the dreams, pleasant eyes
hiding realms of unreason.

Mountains concealing molten rock, runt trees
with poisoned leaves.

He walks from wall to wall, touching
the white walls.

Gummy tendrils grow from his eyes, the earth
is magnified.

He reads you could saunter through Troy
in two minutes.

It is December. The Lord is born.
The world is dead.

IT IS A CITY

Jewelly plastic shining in the machine's remove,
painful ladies striding in antimony, o
in the weeds the wet sod of war clotted
lies with pickerel eyes, with pickerel eyes
and a pike's glossy brown lungs gulping watery air –

it is a city in the muck of sharp mud,
life's stinging black slime
warm against ankles as they rise and fall,
while on the naked shoulder-blades
casual insects auction death away –

a city! Filled with sodden books,
beautiful girls with jewelly hips, filled
with admiring fishy smiles and miles
of coppery machines, enemies dead
or with bad teeth, preposterous dreams
of what had been and familiar schemes:

o Shining creation, when will you die
among the fishbones and the plastic weeds,
and let me lie?

NO PLEASURE

There is no pleasure anywhere.
The zinc air stinks
with a persistent pain. Cheap drugs
rain into the stomach,
becoming mud. The tug
of gravity produces cramps;
I lug myself along like a garden slug
in this damp bed. Nothing I'd read
prepared me for a body this unfair.

As I lift up a coffeecup
I hear the shoulder's intimation
with common fear: I will rip you,
my muscles are on you. And the back too
slips in: Do not bend or I will fit
into your sleep tonight and wake you up
with frightened cramps; there are ramps
into a sea down which we can drive you,
with no one there to shrive you.

Forming letters with a pen
when this treachery
reaches me is my only male answer:
trying not to be
immediate, but in some way elegant
by hand – something my corpse
can't do. But even here
the styleless jerk intrudes,
and I am left alone with it again.

SHE

She starts to grow tears, chemical beast
shut in a dark room with the walls closing
behind her eyelids, all touches hateful,
the white sweep of clean snow death to her,
the grey naked trees death to her.

Her face swells. Tears
slide like glycerine down the round cheeks
and shimmer on her chin. No motion
escapes her face; sadness gathers
in her bones; her fingers curl, an ulcer
pins her down, rotting in her body.

The quiet shadows on the screen
dance, gesticulate, the news comes on and goes,
cars are sold, women sing and smile,
but she does not. Still the tears
run down without a sound. She curls
on her couch; she moves a bit, moves heavily,
as if she had forgotten how.

She moves. The snow shines through the window,
a phosphorescent sea, gleaming;
the etched ghosts of the night sway slightly.

The grass is dead. In spring
it will not be the same, the trees
with their sticky shiny leaves will only be
in costume, mocking, the fresh air
will lie; animals stretching in their skins
stretch to die. But she moves.

She moves. Her shoulders ache. She feels
the harnesses she lives in, she feels
the jelly on her skeleton, she feels the tears
upon her face and dries them with her hands,
touches her hair, sits up and tries to smile.

It is a brave attempt, saying: See how brave I am!
Her breasts hang heavy on her, and the room is dark.

NOTES FROM AND AMONG THE WARS

1

Your drink is twice as strong as mine is
Your mouth is twice as fair as mine is
Your hair is sweeter than mine is
You smile where I could wish to smile
You sleep when I could wish to sleep

I wish to dream, I wish to dream
through our centuries of blood

2

Dead arrogant kings
   bearded in gold
beautiful to archaeologists
living on slaves slaves –
   my people
having come out of Asia
your sons the seven Osmanli mutes
   who strangle and smile
what have you done
but bow and wait
for the petty lords of creation
heirs of the floods and the plagues
   and dead with gold
a crust on the rotted faces
till you after some centuries or so
could use a new plow to conquer Europe?

3

Were the bunks neat in Auschwitz?
Was the soul's blond efficiency repulsed
by the messy blankets of Jews and Gypsies? – If
they had blankets, those who surrendered
immortal teeth of gold, surrendered rings, piles
of prosthetics tabulated in the avenues
between the wooden huts, and all else?

4

In the end you don't even know yourself
only the hill you must climb; but not even
the hill; a bump on it, one hump of grass
a flint, a blade thin in the wind as you climb
each step, each breath taken in a dissimilar time

5

And how after each little separation
we seem to have to learn again
to know each other as awkward strangers do –
the slightest kiss our accidental hands our eyes
that waver off each other as if we had not been
nakedly in love

6

I would like to whistle softly in your ear
to recall to you a tune we might have played
if I could remember it. Instead I sit reading
of man's perpetual wars,
of how he says he strides toward the stars

7

Among the wars
the poet walks along
in his mind
from the start
gone wrong
unable to find
some simple part
that he might make
into an easy song
or phrase to take
as medicine
when he walks along
in his mind,

when his mind soars
from the start,
gone wrong

8

And to see men
attempting to do things
and their women
wary, protecting them,
wolves distrusting all strangers,
smiling like guards

9

As among the wars
and fears
we sail
or kill –
wanderers….

10

And what one would have thought
to have brought forward
to build on
                                has become one's life,
with no addition

11

Movie

There's a man inside there, dying
as you in your homogalactic excitement watch
the fuming awkward plane
fifty-five funny years ago
dive in twisty smoke
into a poison sea of shell-ploughed earth;
it is a movie.
                                     For you it would be much more bitter
just to walk in the streets
than to watch those older deaths again

12

Today when the sun does not rise
Today when the rulers cannot stop the snow
Today as the murders cross the screen
Today as the headlines are hopelessly accepted
Today watching a real-life neo-gothic fistfight
Today on the outskirts of no novel
Today during the shakiness of human life
Today during our constant killing ignorance
declaring our deaths in continuous rehearsal
we live and try to love –
                                        ourselves at least,
if no others

13

The green trees grow from year to year
and seem to have no thoughts
although I hear it said
they scream when we kill before them

14

And give us a little pity too:
for the last drink in the whisky bottle
sunday afternoon, for the calcium in our spines
for the daily prejudiced paper, the constant liars
those who think war is a high-school debate
the ones who take freedom away
in the name of freedom
as our portions get smaller

Forgive us: for whom civilization consists of acquiring
the correct mental addictions, those of us who act
as if we hated the human in ourselves
knowing there is enough to hate
in the human in ourselves

The wars the slaveries no dead men redeemed by poems
no humiliation redressed with songs
no chain scars in the soul erased with apologies
a hundred years late
the simple everyday savagery of parent to child
or child to parent brother to brother sister to sister

The torture goes on forever as we in perpetual motion
breed and destroy ourselves for any reason
even intelligent ones

All of which we have always known
in despair and amusement at ourselves

15

And there is an egypt of the mind
grotesque mysterious remote
sacrificial
where the dunes are piling and unpiling
their arabesques coiling about some point
not grasped some
secret living to be learned
desperately longed for....

Blue and green commingling, the muscley sea
sliding through the mind, a notion of deeper rivers
than those that run over the earth, among the stars
currents in the bright mixture pulsing, something
that might be there to save us as it seems
we cannot save ourselves or do not want to....

16

To be willingless, to be willing….

Willingless and willing, as when
the pickup truck went around
a slight curve to the right
years ago and stopped. Off the road
a small triangular piece of level ground
a wooden shack a quick shallow river
and then the trees again as far as could be seen
night coming thoughts of bears the sound
of crisp leaves as bits of wind brushed off them
a place unknown and feared
and the driver saying This
is as far as I go
meaning this is as far as you go….

17

But what should we expect of our memories
except remembrance? We who are so adept
so practiced in false hopes so able to read
the slightest changes in a face
the slightest intonations in a voice
the indications of things
that do not exist affirmations
never considered by the other….

18

But me? Waking up mornings
my mouth full of blood
it seeming to be such a difficult life
and yet so easy not to be
as water rings in the musical hillside sewers
in a false Spring
hoarding regrets

And the ghost that sings in my blood
a mortal
everything waiting for its boat-shaped grave ender
of the sad tricks we play on ourselves
ender of foolish lives
and foolish loves greatly desired ending
the crying instruments of speech
that repeat and repeat themselves happily repeating
the past from which they are trying to rise

19

You smile where I could wish to smile
You sleep when I could wish to sleep….
It is not the milk-bearing tree I see
but the one that seeps blood or trees
exploding like tnt in the winter's cold

20

Caught in the maze of life
and knowing only that we end

Avoiding infinity
with questions

Was I a lover you had
out of your kindliness
in wintertime?

Is today the day I got old?

Is today the day you got old?
And were only able to sing a structured song?
So –

If you were in the air
would you be a bird?
If you were able
would you wish to be?
And would you sing
if you wished to be?
And if you cared to be –

Would you want to fly? knowing
below and as you fly
in the green concealed pit
the hunters with their sighted shotguns lie.

LIKE A RIVER

And after flowing into the prairie sunset the big plane settled
to earth as though it were contented in this bowl.
The raiders no longer ride over. Their horses are small now,
used for bareback races at country rodeos. Drunks in the hot sun
whoop and bet a dollar at random on Indians.

Before stolen horses were gained from the South, before
the muskets came in the West, before trade-liquor,
Fort Whoop-Up, before a man could own land forever,
himself alone, if he were white, the bands drifted,
small families moved on foot in wintertime.

It is a lonely place for all of us when the snow curls
and we cannot see from house to house,
if there are houses to see. The cities themselves seem fenced,
as if surrounded by wire as farms are, marked off,
concentration camps of the soul.

How many signs must be known, how many curves recalled
to prove the traveller's still on the earth he thinks he is? –
not driving by some sudden unnoticed mistake
through Outer Mongolia, the Argentinian pampas,
nearing an unfamiliar, ruined city in Africa?

We wander. It is our way. The people with whom we have no
    relation
went also, they on regular trails in search of food,
we on highways, railways, in planes, hungry with curiosity,
forgetting as soon as we learn, wanting rest
and ownership, something in which to believe for once.

The plane will go up and on to another separate city
from which the sunset flows like a river into the blackening sky;
we will go on, until we are gone. And on the prairie
the ghosts who own it continue to walk in clans,
searching for food and for what they once knew.

THE FIRST BIRD OF SPRING

Cheerfully he tells a lie about seeing Spring's first bird.

Doesn't he know that the discoloured chickadees stayed all Winter in the snow, hopping from one discarded seed to another?

Doesn't he know that those now transparent birds are invisible in the watery March air, invisible to all others but himself – and that they can never be the first since they are always there?

It is some other bird he thinks of, some presence other than that of those scattered multitudes of tiny souls encased in bone.

The bird he thinks of he thinks of at night.

It is huge. It stands on a dark bank of snow at the corner of the house, shadowed. Its feathers are black swords.

It is of this bird that the man forges a document.

I saw the first bird of Spring he says, leading his hearers to think of chickadees or to think of the resurgent robins who carry dried blood stains on their breasts.

UNTIL IT WAS YELLOW.

from the Romanian of Geo Dumitrescu

It may have been the cart of memories
passing by; but through the thick dust
the girl's quivering silhouette
no longer could be seen
on the disc of the earth giddily whirled
until it was yellow.

It may have been that your crying
came from wine, came from lost tears; the rains
always come down in the wake of departing cranes.
It may have been; and on the envelope,
in the corner, the many-coloured butterfly,
a stamp: your involuntary kiss.

Less than that what can there be? –
Autumn's garden, Autumn drunk in the mud,
her hair all wet, provocative,
laughing in her damp intimate make-up
at your wooden disguise.

In vain, in vain. You will never find
the forest ring once thrown away –
round itself the tree gathers
new rings of gold as the tree shakes off
blue acorns.

Beware of dying – hate the chalk
in the white hour. Autumn
will give you a little
needed despondency. It may have been
the cart of memories passing by,
your involuntary kiss, a butterfly….

DREAM

Bees won't fly when it's this cold;
sixty degrees is what they need.

Wings freeze. A hundred miles beyond
the white frontier the European honey bee

frightens the natives. They know it;
it moves ahead. Wings freeze, though.

In winter one Indian
moves slowly through the snow,
hoping for sweetness, a taste.

DREAM

The lone figure leans in the snow.
A rifle is stuck beside him:
one hand is on it.

He waits an approaching figure.
He will decide, when it comes,
to kill or to run.

It is the white centre of the world
his reason squats in.

COMPLAINT

You don't tell me much about the presents
  strange oriental men give you –
the twelve small dolls in a box,
  the tiny bowl of asparagus sprouts,
their thin green shoots pointing to the sky.

EVERYWHERE I GO

What are people talking about. Everywhere I go they whisper.

They stick their eyes at me, right at the base of the breastbone, when I'm not looking.

The breastbone seems flat, pointed like a dagger to the top of my stomach.

O, my stomach, my stomach…when the knife rips you open it will find coffee and four strips of bacon, pieces of chewed beard and a handwritten note saying I have left town forever again.

WHY DO YOU HATE ME?

So you live of the sea;
and I am the dry acrid land.

You have the sweet fish swimming
and dull mannerly grain grows in me.

Your blood shines in curving darts;
I grow in calculated rows.

So I say I love you,
and you say, Why do you hate me?

I speak in a foreign language.
You don't know what I say.

BLUE COW PHRASES

If I'm disgusted with my life I'm disgusted with yours too.

All we do is invent blue cow phrases dripping thin vapid milk.

Everything is history to us, even the future. As if they were accomplished we denigrate the slim tubular aluminum cities and the rigid creatures descended from us who in them follow their daily routes through computed mazes.

History is horrible, remembrance is horrible, time is horrible.

Everything we recall is told on a flat page and becomes something else in telling, not less but else. The gold sea is wrenched to our purpose, the chocolate earth is wrenched to our purpose, the red sky is wrenched to our purpose....

Rows of identical people are stacked in closets in the remaining forests, waiting to steal our names.

IN THE CRAMMED WORLD

1. Tired, unsure, fearing war, in the crammed world surrounded,
leafless trees rising from the cold ground, a man
stoops as the grey slatted sky presses down,
unwilling to think of the possible facts of a future day.

Nights are spent among the seductive beasts, smiling and calling,
each earnest as a rock. Dreams rise and waver, slipslide,
echoing the stonegreen undersea they represent themselves as,
filled with weeds, cutting reefs, long strips of slit muscle
contracting silently. Teeth are scattered on the cool sand, not shells.

This is the region of the bleak weasel, ribby, at the shore. He sneaks
through the blind landscape sniffing blood among the useless vegetables;
wind sprays the tall grass stalks with poisons from the yellow air;
somewhere there a weak face smiles carefully.

Under water or above not success nor failure inhabits the dreams;
only fear, too near to be unwelcome always. The mind
scares itself with spectres more friendly than the world of smoke:
one may escape from them, not from concrete and jails.

2. A man starved of something he will not admit admires his skinniness,
in sorrow; each exposed bone is an honourable medal. He says, Comfort
my sad eyes. It is pleasure I want from your proffered breast,
not that thin gruelly milk that drips from the nipple.
Accept my suffering, which is all I have made of my life,
which is all the love I want to offer you.

3. Painful man, your hurt lasts longer than a movie;
it will not amuse a woman or the future for so long. New turns
must be invented every day. And never tricks. So dream; dream of success,
and hope, though hope for what you cannot guess, but when you slide
with your eyes closed into the universe you invented viciously,
do not complain that the wrong doors open wide, open, wait,
then close behind you,
and some friendly animal long thought of greets you and grows fat
lapping your red gore.

A LONG CONTINUAL ARGUMENT WITH MYSELF

As if human beings only lived one moment at a time!
– no past, no future; as if a part of the pain
of receiving that simple act of kindness
were not the memory of it occurring before –

as if there were nothing to hope for
when a stranger woman smiles and kisses you
at someone else's kitchen door, as if
that tree of gratitude for humans would not bloom again –

which will:
silver in the silver sun.

From *THE GREEN PLAIN, 1979*

THE GREEN PLAIN

Small human figures and fanciful monsters
abound. Dreams surround us,
preserve us. We praise constancy as brave,
but variation's lovelier.

Rain surrounds us, arguments and dreams, there are
forests between us, there are
too many of us for comfort, always were.

Is civilization
only a lack of room, only
an ant-heap at last? – the strutting cities
of the East, battered gold,
the crammed walls of India,
humanity swarming, indistinguishable
from the earth?

Even the nomads roaming the green plain, for them
at last no land was ever enough.

Spreading – but now we can go anywhere
and we are afraid
and talk of small farms instead of the stars
and all the places we go
space is distorted.

How shall we save the symmetry of the universe? –
or our own symmetry, which is the same.

Which myths
should capture us, since we do not wish
to be opened, to be complete? –
or are they all the same, all of them?

Now a dream involves me, of a giant sprawled among stars,
face to the dark, his eyes closed.
Common.

Only he is not breathing, he does not heave.
Is it Gulliver? – huge, image of us, tied, webbed in,
and never learning anything,

always ignorant,
always amazed, always capable of delight,
and giving it, though ending in hatred, but
an image only. Of disaster. But there is no disaster.
It is just that we lose joy and die.

But is there a symmetry?

Is there reason
in the galaxies – Or is this all glass,
a block bubbled in a fire, accident only,
prettiness fused without care, pettiness,
though some logic, alien but understandable,
in the ruined crystal?

The forests, the forests, swaying,
there is no reason why they should be beautiful.
They live for their own reasons, not ours.
But they are.

It is not time that flows but the world.

And the world flows,
still flows. Even in these worn-out days,
worn-out terms,
once in a while our poets
must
speak

of Spring! Of all things! The flowers
blow in their faces too, and they smell perfumes,
and they are seduced
by colour – rural as the hairy crocus or urban as a waxy tulip.

But confusion. The world
flows past. It is hard to remember age. Does
this always world flow? Does it? Please say it does,
not time.
Do not say time flows.
Say: We do. Say: We live.

Fly-speck, fly-speck. In this ever island Earth
we are the tiny giants, swaggering
behind the dinosaurs, lovely,
tame brontosaurus, sweet cows lumbering
among the coal trees, fronds offering
shade and future fuel.

And the land around us green and happy,
waiting as you wait for a killer to spring,
a full-sized blur,
waiting like a tree in southern Saskatchewan,
remarked on, lonely and famous as a saint.

The mechanisms by which the stars generate invention
live all over and around us
and yet we refine machines, defer
to tricks as discovery. Everything is always here,
and burning.

There are no surprises, there is only
what is left. We live
inside the stars,

burning, burning,
the mechanisms.

Stars, rain, forests.
Stars rain forests.
Sew up the lives together. There is
this only world. Thank God: this World
and its wrapped variations
spreading around and happy, flowing,
flowing through the climate of intelligence,
beautiful confusion looking around,
seeing the mechanics and the clouds
and marvelling, O Memory….

From THE NIGHT THE DOG SMILED, 1986

DRIVING

You never say anything in your letters. You say,
I drove all night long through the snow
in someone else's car
and the heater wouldn't work and I nearly froze.
But I know that. I live in this country too.
I know how beautiful it is at night
with the white snow banked in the moonlight.

Around black trees and tangled bushes,
how lonely and lovely that driving is,
how deadly. You become the country.
You are by yourself in that channel of snow
and pines and pines,
whether the pines and snow flow backwards smoothly,
whether you drive or you stop or you walk or you sit.

This land waits. It watches. How beautifully desolate
our country is, out of the snug cities,
and how it fits a human. You say you drove.
It doesn't matter to me.
All I can see is the silent cold car gliding,
walled in, your face smooth, your mind empty,
cold foot on the pedal, cold hands on the wheel.

THE CITIES WE LONGED FOR

In summer we were disappointed
with the open. We had stood
the winter, hoping for stronger winds
to prove our worth;
this was a foolish pride,
as good as any other.

But in the summer we were discontented
with the easiness, not being accustomed
to freedom, and it was
the cities we longed for,
the fabulous, the anonymous,
not the summer but the rush.

It was the cities we entered
instead of entering manhood;
and we never saw a thing, I least of all,
until one day my eyes opened briefly.

Then it was disgust I saw,
it was fear of ourselves I saw,
so that we ceased to live and only moved,
and my eyes closed
and I wrote sweet lyrics,
la la la la la....

Then I was angry, foolishly,
for not having seen, I wanted to cry:
Burn your delicious cars,
Crush down the electric towers,
Throw out the mechanisms
that work so well
until they die, no love
until they die.

It was too late. My eyes
were closed. Freedom, summer,
never seemed to be what we wanted.

THE PERMANENT TOURIST COMES HOME

1. To the oppressed
nothing is left but song,
which the rich will adopt in a more melodious form.
Even your voice will be stolen from you
and the rhythm of your chains will be modulated
by choirs of celestial beings – which is necessary:
okay, okay, obey,
since your only function is to die.

2. Speak.
Speak. But be careful of making moulds
which the spiritually illiterate
can fill up with gumbo.

3. Guarded and guided,
the fact before the hypothesis: early morning,
somewhere in the time
that I was, this simple apparition –
my small mother, orange flannel nightgown,
early light. Wee Willie Winkie, her finger
to her lips, walks in slow motion
on her delicate ankles,
sibilant, saying Shh, shh,
Father's dead.

4. I wake up
and sit on the edge of the bed.
You sparrow, mother, you beautiful sparrow.

5. I love you. Father is not dead.
Time is dead. There is a scoop in time
whatever self my self is
returns to every time, my grey sweet mother.

6. Well, to die in the Spring
and be buried in the muck
seems reasonable. Enough
of this. The mountains are bright tonight
outside my window, and passing by.
Awkwardly, I am in love again.

ROCKS, WOODS, SEAS

The ground that looks so firm is bog,
that ground is death, corpses lurk in it,
dead houses. The city is quiet, not thinking,
where
is everyone? Today?

The forest had seemed full of people in their various skins,
it was as if the malevolent bears
could at least be reasoned with, the deer
able to discuss their fears, defending
a dangerous way of life. When we think cold we feel cold.
It is the same, they would say.
When we feel cold we think cold.

But where is everyone?
Isn't there anything but cigarettes in this city,
red marks in the night, isn't there anything
besides the cars that crawl
along their crowded routes, tunnels,
and painful buildings, is there nothing
but me after all? Did I dream this,
this world – all there is?

I had thought of rocks,
of green, I had thought
of shells, I was the one who had considered wood,
seas, animals flexing,
that was it: I had thought of humans,
pitiful and pleasing in their disease of life,
disease of time, disease of strife;
but there was no one here but me at all,
on this ground.

CONCERNING STARS, FLOWERS, LOVE, ETC.

Make it easier, they say, make it easier. Tell
me something I already know, about stars or flowers or,
or happiness. I am happy sometimes, though
not right now, specially. Things are not going
too good right now. But you should try
to cheer people up, they say. There is
a good side to life, though
not right now, specially. Though the stars
continue to shine in some places and the flowers
continue to bloom in some places
and people do not starve in some places
and people are not killed in some places
and there are no wars in some places
and there are no slaves in some places
and in some places people love each other,
they say. Though I don't know where. They say,
I don't *want* to be sad. Help me not to know.

BIG MIRROR

I am in dentist's chair leaning back.

You are evil dentist banging on tools.
Opening and shutting drawers in cabinets.

You're toothchipper sliding around behind me.

You conferring behind hand.
Whispering to nurse about me.

You hate my teeth.

I know her too.

But you the one hustling in and out of room.
Killing time jingling instruments.
Rattling sheets x-ray film adjusting lights.
Waiting for me to be afraid so you can begin.

What use hurting me if not afraid?
Job must have other compensation than monetary.

I know you fat face no hair on head.
Soft red bulging lips estimating me.

I know you blotched purple and white skin face.
I know trembly hand waiting with excitement
to rape mouth of me.

I know what needles and chrome in there
you want to stick.

I am I said in dentist's chair leaning back.

There on ceiling stand upside-down
black transparent flies immobilized in horror
at what you going to do to me.

You never pulled fly's tooth.
You never pulled fly's tooth.

Black flies never knowing what like
to have long tooth roots drawn slow out of jaw.
Feel hard part of body suctioned out of body.

Long pull not know.

But feel sorry for me sitting in dentist's chair.
Horrified you bald man dentist.

Short white coat dentist in background always.

Head of me bolted so can't turn or discover
secret dirty work only mind knows.

Start soon now getting scared.

What you will do to me with help smiling blonde
nurse receptionist bleach maybe too much.
Greasy lipstick red on big mouth grinning.
Hate men except fat dentist sometimes who hurts.
Pays money to buy javex lipstick.

Sorry of flies no good.

Ridiculous caught in dentist's chair looking at ceiling.
Painted green reflects light.

Big mirror on cabinet in corner can see from corner of eye
self and look dumb tied rigormortis here
and gagged cotton snick machine
takes inside wrong picture on other side of room.

Snick estimates me.

I am safe look like pay insurance.
Or work and will grunt hurt and screw up eyes good.

Evil damn dentist comes fast around
left side of chair holding weapons.

Now start fat man.

YUKICHI FUKUZAWA

I turned away astonished with my own face
full of tears and beer on my breath. My
enemies smiled to each other and decided
to be kind.
                Why does this fool love?
I sit sad   quiet   like a priest
doing penance. I was bold
when I was young.
I should hide from my brothers.

O
bigoted saints
who fear to act and distress others
there are no police for your souls.
You will live to eat the adulation
of those who put up with you
because of your age.

The golden fish curl around the trees
the branches   waiting. Be
a happy child.

You know people wait for you to die.
I will take bitter medicine.
This hardship is pleasure.

RETURN TRAIN

A low, empty-
looking, unpainted house;
back of it, the corn
blighted, the tractor
abandoned.

LIKE WATER

I wish my love could
be taken for granted.

It's just there like water,
always present, unfrozen.

This is not to be a desert
we inhabit.

REPORT ON ABSENCE

Well, it's full of your poems, my life,
those oases I never thought I'd need,
and resentments towards your enemies,
as if I hadn't made enough of my own.
A couple of nights ago a friend visited me,
he's a good young poet, though
I don't know what young means any more, dammit,
I miss you, oasis: that I thought I
would never need.

SVEJK

Svejk said, 'marjoram
smells like an ink-bottle
          in a valley of flowering acacias.
On the hill….'
                    A clerk interrupted
imploringly, the smell
(my dear the smell was dreadful) floated
in the wooden office.
                         God,
the furniture was beautiful.
                              If
only
there
were
woman
in it, in the bottle, in the breeze.

COLD, HEAT

Life gets more extreme as it goes on.
I don't remember these temperatures
going up and down so much
when I was younger. God:
am I going to die?

Then, the heat was only heat,
the cold, cold. Now
every bone aches with questions.

SHAKESPEARE'S SONNETS

I'm not interested in rainbows
but in the sky itself, the serene
not the spectacular: the permanent.

This is a business of trying to make things permanent,
not ephemeral. What else to do?
We know we die, so chase notoriety too.

All the couples of Shakespeare's sonnets
make sense to me. It was another love
other than the Dark One he reached for.

Us.

INSECT HOPES

The world's longest poem didn't start like this
didn't go on like this
it doesn't end like this – there was still
a cigarette burning. After
the ending, after all the Indians
the Pygmies, the Gypsies, the Jews
the burned and the black and the spurned
after all the cheated and demeaned were buried by bulldozers
or sold as cheap souvenirs in green translucent glass
that cigarette still fumed –
what wealth!

And the writer of all that stuff
was still stupid
he still thought that when people said
I understand
they understood

he didn't know that he lied for pleasure
others, profit
and he still saw
all-around wrap-around death and didn't believe it
and woke up one night in the maw and believed it

Knowing what was wanted

Not these sweaty visions everyone has
no recognizable rhythms
no beauty in the line
no knowledge
                    only noise
no feeling of pain

This whole civilization is noise
we are not wholly beasts yet
but the politicians roar at us
until civilization is minor

And we are surrounded by liars
so that when the poet that is in us says
we are surrounded by liars
he is called a liar
or is given prizes, liar
obligations

O I am sick and called sick
and I am healthier than you are

At least I know how lovely we are

Enduring –

Which is history
we are one after the other
we are the stars of this show
but we are
at the end of all time

What nonsense we talk
What nonsense we're told
What nonsense we are

But I wanted to tell you still how lovely we are
of the ages of jewels
of failed cities
of the notion that there was good
how this century began like all the others

in blood
and milk-white dreams
and ended
with insect hopes
with insect hopes
all in a heap
like all the others
who ever died

FIVE POEMS AFTER SANSKRIT

1. A stranger sings in the village at night:
listening to the heavy sound of clouds:
black in a sullen sky: tears in his eyes:
he sings a song of his loneliness: his longing.

The listeners to those nearby sounds know
how like death distance from a lover is:
how like death: even pride is forgotten:
they too even refuse to say goodbye to it.

2. Black smoke from a dirty fire:
these clouds: covering the whole
sky: and the fresh thick grass is
a dark mat on the earth: it
is the time for love: when those
who are alone must sing their
songs softly: only to death.

3. Alone in her husband's house she hears
from far away the slow warm spring
vibrating sound of black bees
moving among the birds –
tremulous music
of love. She hears
shyly, so
shyly
longs
:

4. Through tears she saw the lovely
masses of clouds
grouping in a dark sky: 'Love,
if you leave me
now…' she said: holding me: her
legs moving: words
turn away helplessly from
what she did then.

5. Like a shy woman showing:
for the first time: in love: her thighs:
the sandy beds of autumn rivers.

SPEECH ABOUT A BLACKFOOT WOMAN WITH TRAVOIS, PHOTO BY R.H. TRUEMAN

ca. 1890

Yes, yes, they never developed the wheel.
Or the gun. Cheap sarcasm. Here is the queen
of the prairie, holding a sad white horse
not by the rein (a string, really) in her hand
but by being there. She is taller than the horse
and darker. Even in her foreign clothes
there is regality. Time for a metaphor. She stares.
The land stretches. That's not a metaphor,
that is the truth. The horizon looks like a line
drawn by Brian Fisher, exact and ambiguous.
She's dead now. I love her. I guess.
Don't like the horse much. It's dead too.

WHITE PHILHARMONIC NOVELS

1. I walked like a cat behind my father.

2. This turbulent ear hears turbulent music,
the poem made up of its parts.

3. I have a picture of her,
smiling

she was smiling at the camera,
not me

She would be in silks
She would be wary & rough
under the sheets (under the stuff)

The boldness of her innocence

You wouldn't care

What do you remember
after you've been happy?

4. The message is that there is no message.
You can't live forever on resentment.

The thing is whether to stuff stuff
into the middle or into
the many endings.

I have a picture,
of you smiling

Single-minded pervert.

My lips are sour and the voice won't speak.

She put on a garment of gaiety and courage
the night the Dog smiled

I myself
am impatient with myself

> I know you don't lie to me
> Your lies are only aimed at yourself,
> the only one you must and can
> not convince. Never believing, you.

INSTRUCTIONS FOR PATIENTS

> Watch out for sharp pieces of bone.

> A poor frail body

She wants to know why her parents
seem like leftovers
from last year

By subdividing ages
of evolutionary stages

> We live in an eternal Now
> the estuaries of an ancient sea
> the past of saints
> and devils & miracles

It is insane to pretend to be insane.

You cannot reveal yourself:
You cannot conceal yourself.

it is necessary only to be relentless

> Stamping your feet like horses –

5. Look, you always gave me
good things, you. Yourself. That you sent me,
trustingly. That I wear like a beautiful
bright silk badge. That I didn't earn, but that
I wear for bravery.

I liked it because I had no other choice,
a dancer out of time.

In the forest
heavy animals move

water, a black trickle of spilt ink
among the blazing rocks –

– habits of description.

No, not yours, you'll say,
and you know you lie
but you have to say.

I wish I were lying with you now. Lovely.
But tried and tired. Taught. And in tears.
Indeed. Freezing.

6. This is about ridges of bone, this
is about the evil your desire does, this
is in the night the Dog smiles,
this is about you.

It is necessary to be relentless.
That can't be the end of it,
still treading the prison corridors
of the empty mountains
Looking
at her and thinking

The train was standing in the station
waiting exactly where I had left it
months earlier,
looking older

Stamping its feet like horses.

Look, what
was once done with passion is now done with love,
and more slowly

This solid rock becomes an open door
in a huge explosion of night

The words slid sideways. Wise.

I kept looking out the window to see
if it was Spring yet,
but Winter was still on the mountains,
looking in the window
to see if I'd grown young yet or if
my hair was dark again

How can I grow up if I never was young?

And then he saw
that he was secure
in his cultivation
of this minute garden.

Oh.

& your belief can't make it true, your
doubt won't make it false

O my largest milieu is belief

Not the end of nature

of living out this life of evil, of desire, of acting

You cannot reveal yourself
You prefer the blood of death
to the blood of birth

She put on a garment

You cannot conceal yourself

She would be

in silks.

The message is that there is no message.

We are part of the tomb itself,
not of the furnishings.

This death is not the end of nature,
but of fault –

These insulted empires
These Cambodias
These Ethiopias

– the expression of sadness on their faces
as they killed

This night the Dog smiled,
strange, brave, and unlucky Comrade

remembering pain almost with affection.

7. The train was standing in
the station, waiting exactly where
it had left us years
earlier, looking older,
stamping its feet

She wants to know why her lovers
look like leftovers

The boldness of her

> Look, nobody gets wise writing
> Now I must be making
> pretty manners
> at you
> It's necessary to realize that all these phrases
> are stolen. The arrangement is all.

You about to turn away,
this is what I almost wanted to say

> The web traps you, not
> others
> – the wounded hills.

His voice coloured. He
felt
something
about Hafez
something about the Chinese
something
romantic.

It's lonely here and I'm going mad.

I'd rather be a toy to you than
nothing at all to you.
I'm not talking to you.

Something he would like to have.
Something she would like to be.

Emotional forgers.

'– beautiful women were moved
to the strongest emotion'

The Tireless Traveller

the tireless traveller says
you never say anything in your letters.

Blue lakes and the mountains
get thirsty too. All the day long.

A low, empty-
looking, unpainted house.
Back of it, the corn
blighted, the tractor
abandoned.

This earth is a body.

He feels
like a giant wrinkled spider spinning his web
for himself
and it is not like sitting on a bus dreaming
of women, she
turned suddenly and kissed him on the mouth
violently and he didn't know what to do in
his shame –

Anxious and asking.
He did not know where her eyes were.
He did not know where his eyes were.

Constantly thinking.
You. In silks.

8. In the edge
of a painful century

Some things are more important than the truth

Life gets more extreme
as it goes on.

I don't remember
these temperatures
going up and down
so much

Yet every bone aches with questions.

'Your mania for sentences
has dried up your heart.'

9. Remember who you are speaking to –

– the strains of the Nutcracker heard
from a radio station on the same frequency
with the countdown
for the first Los Alamos test –

This turbulent ear hears turbulent news
We will not bow to an obscene law

I will piss on the elegant
and join you in your undersized armies.
I know you will lose.
We all do.
But you have your excuses

Atlas of Ancient Dreads

Atlas of Ancient Youth
Atlas of Ancient Lust
You have your excuses

You need someone to lead you to ruin,
but I'm not the one. See the neighbours.

No one could name all their griefs.

Train wheels going shut up, shut up, shut up

10. The horse sinks knee deep
in silk
in America and the muck
the bruised flesh of the meadows
where politicians do not walk
stamping their feet like trains.

This is unsupportable.

I made these voices.

The arrangement is all.

It grew and grew until it was bigger than I was
and it made me think that I was bigger than I was.

The lie is elaborate and exact.

The cold miser sits chittering
in the old kitchen.
What good is a witness
who will not tell his tale?

& now I must wash and go.

I love you.

THE WEATHER

I'd like to live a slower life.
The weather gets in my words
and I want them dry. Line after line
writes itself on my face, not a grace
of age but wrinkled humour. I laugh
more than I should or more
than anyone should. This is good.

But guess again. Everyone leans, each
on each other. This is a life
without an image. But only
because nothing does much more
than just resemble. Do the shamans
do what they say they do, dancing?
This is epistemology.

This is guesswork, this is love,
this is giving up gorgeousness to please you,
you beautiful dead to be. God bless
the weather and the words. Any words. Any weather.
And where or whom. I'd never taken count before.
I wish I had. And then
I did. And here
the weather wrote again.

From APOLOGY FOR ABSENCE, 1993

BEING CAUGHT *(Author's preface to Apology for Absence)*

I was born in Regina, Saskatchewan, in 1938. I can remember very little of my life. What I do remember I am suspicious of. I may have invented it.

Was I told that I would not drink any milk except goat's milk and that this was discovered at the last moment? Did I nearly die?

My mother was short, small, thin, immensely interesting. I did not understand that there were fathers.

In Yellow Grass, Saskatchewan, as I lay on a couch in the parlour with jaundice and my stuffed kangaroo I found out that my mother was a teacher. She must have been very different from the teachers I had encountered that year, my first year in school. On the very first day I realized that they were trying to tell me what to do. I ran away, but they caught me. They have been catching me ever since.

The doctor looked at my stuffed toy. He said, I see you've got a kangaroo. I said, No. I haven't got Roo. He shook his head. My mother smiled.

Sometime that spring I stepped on a nail in a board. I clumped to the house crying, the nail fixing the board to my foot like a paleolithic ski. My mother comforted me but it wasn't pain or the blood that made me cry. I didn't know how to get the board off my foot and I felt awkward and stupid.

When I was in grade three I had a dog.

When I was in grade four the boys spoke Russian when they wanted to leave me out.

We lived happily ever after, it seemed to me, a family of fabulists, for seven or eight years. We were happy; I was not. Then everything fell apart again.

It is not the dead that dying hurts most.

****

I don't know how I came to write. I don't know. One day, it seemed, I was, desperately, as if I were trying to explain the world, or bits of it, to myself. And to others eventually. That is what I thought.

Now I think that I am only trying to model tiny bits of a world too wide and too various and too frightening to be comprehended by anything but lies.

I love words and therefore I am a liar.

Playing this fatal game of hide and seek never seems to stop.

****

Once upon a time a poet and a woman were lying on a bed. The woman was very beautiful. She was younger than the poet and he was much younger than she was. They were quarrelling softly. Moonlight shone through the open window. You don't love me, you don't love anyone, she said. All you love is words and watching people and writing things down, she said. All you do is watch.

No. No, he said.

You don't, she said.

That's not true, he said.

He was leaning on his right arm, leaning half over her. A tear slid down her cheek and the moonlight caught it. Her eyes were open. The poet got off the bed, turned, ran naked to his desk.

You see, you see, the woman said.

****

Years later the man was remembering his mother's death. He had not been there. He had loved his mother and he loved his mother. He wrote down, for himself, She died brave and poor and worn out. That's what I feel, he thought. But I can't put it in here unless it's really true.

****

I like to make pretty shapes, pretty things. I can hear them. I wish I could offer consolation, if not to others at least to myself. I am trying to hold the world together.

I want to be at home in the weather.

I know that I am confused.

What to make of it all?

John Newlove, 1993

AUTOBIOGRAPHY

I am a technician of the absurd,
I am a comedian of death.

I am the man your mother warned you against,
I am the man my mother warned me against.

AUTOBIOGRAPHY

I used to think that I was just like you.
Then I started writing poems.

They took years to teach me
that I was right.

GOD BLESS THE BEAR

How many of them die of old age?
They die of the tension of not-knowing,
the apprehension.
                    Fear sits in their guts,
thus the courage, the quickness, the shyness
of a deer asking Are you my death? the gopher
taking one last look. I want to know
what my death looks like
no matter how fast it comes.

Or the bear. God bless the bear,
arthritic as me, doing its death-clown act
on two legs, ready to embrace, saying
I'm just you in funny clothes.
Your clothes are funny too. Let's wrestle,
my little man, my little son, my little death, my brother.

AUTOBIOGRAPHY

Embraces turned friendly,
the friendly kiss on the cheek
 – God damn friendship! –
and life became normally normal.

AUTOBIOGRAPHY

Always the neglected lover,
always the forlorn lover confessing
to an empty hall, an empty hell.

Everything comes out of everything.
I just live in this world,
I don't know much about it.

POEM WITH RAVENS

Dease Lake to Watson Lake
November 1985

And with a penetrating silence
and with solitary gestures,
an oil drum among the pines,
and with good gravel roads
and with an understanding of itself
that is not to be understood
and with pines
and with cheeseburgers
and with mock log cabins
and with real ones
and with an acceptance of the inside world
that is to be understood
and is not solitary or a gesture
and with an understanding of light
and with pines and pines
refusing to leave home,
one bowing gracefully like a geisha,
and with comfortable immensities
and with a quiet pride kidding the outsiders
gently and gently and gently and gently
and with pines and with pride
and, yes, with snow, we must mention snow
where colour itself seems a type of wealth
and with danger and with pines
and with serenity and with calmness
and with pines and with pines and with pines
and with humans, always with humans....

SUCH FUN, SUCH FUN

When the poets stopped writing poetry
I thought they were dead
and I went about and tried to describe my country
not leaf by leaf but soul by soul
and I found that though my soul was obscure
it was common. Liquor cured me or calmed me
and pain and long lying lines.

And the poets came back to life and said I was a poet too
and I was astonished!
I hadn't thought they'd known so much
or that I had cared so much.

And the booze tastes good even if the body aches
and the end is shame – but the sheer pleasure
of the gift, of a few gloomy words –

This is prose, this is a ghost with a steel chisel
sneaking another letter onto the stone.

Such fun, such fun. I guess you would have to pay attention
to someone besides yourself. It's better to celebrate
your funeral before you die.

Thank you, thank you.

AUTOBIOGRAPHY

This job is making my voice shrill.
It used to grumble along
like an old movie.

It calmed bartenders.
Now even women don't trust me.

PROGRESS

Up to a white world and it's still snowing.
    Violence is reported but I didn't catch the details,
time for breakfast. My letter is in the newspaper,
    dancing to someone else's loony tunes.

Bugdancing. That's the thing in town right now
    and I think I'd better get going. Cabin-fever
and the forty-foot stare are getting me nowhere
    but down and out. It doesn't look like up

to me. And so the distress, this distress,
    opens like a slowly-photographed flower growing
into a velvet-wrinkled colour, centred in itself
    brightly, all alone. Stick it in your mind.

I seem to be losing my life. I don't
    care, I'm on nobody's side, not even my own,
I don't care for this place full of mumbling old men,
    vain, fingering their eccentricities

like me. I want to forget my past selves
    who cried out in pain out of their rationality,
explaining everything, understanding nothing,
    factual, weighted by false continents.

What has a Europe got to do with me? –
    huge itching blood clot millennially slaughtering
itself so that generations fled insane from the plague
    of culture, carrying the infection.

Snow covers the scars for a moment, sun
    glitters without giving life to the philharmonia
of the endless earth I grew up on. Now mountains
    choke me, postcards next to me stifling me.

Into the plane, into the train, into
    anything including my bruised, used, abused brain,
that modeller of truth, trampler on reality,
    fabricating any world to live in

except the one it does, these landscapes, this
    body stumbling dumbly under itself, wanting
to leave, wanting to stay, wavering like a weed
    in the water. These weeds are flowers too.

We haven't found a use for all of them.
    No flowers in this whiteness except cut ones in vases,
silk flowers in department stores, blood flowers blooming
    vaguely in flesh. Where is this taking me?

Bring in the Spring by yourselves! This shabby
    muddy dawn has nothing to do with me, I have
too much of a longing for colour, for green,
    to endure this slow mixture easily.

The mountains are remotely drifting by
    outside my window and, beneath the floating plane,
the notched scenery, ragged, unsentimental,
    without content. Once there was silver here.

Unsentimental: unlike the people,
    who infest the land with their wandering dreams
of peace and certitude, over which they quarrel
    communally, incessantly angry.

The dinosaur plane dashes on, fleeing east,
    first to the empty prairie airport full
of strangers being remotely polite to each other.
    This is not a journey to satisfy

my own curiosity at my own
    cargo. It is merely a trip, a temporary
escape, a hallucination of the freedom
    I cannot have and will not comprehend.

Why do I keep thinking of dead flowers,
    silk flowers, nylon flowers, she wore purple
flowers? There was nothing alive to the flowers
    except her underneath them. Who was she?

Who is *she*? I don't know. Only the wisps
    of memory tempt me to go further. I don't
want to. I would rather remember my father
    scratching his back like a bear on the door.

Who was he? I don't know. Back into
    the metal cocoon at 32,000 feet,
quarantined in the sky with water and rye.
    No one can walk in to analyse me.

Everything is a result of forcing.
    It is a makeshift world. What structure holds me
together? A coloured disease, a silk flower
    called life? Or the mere relativity

of the truth? Remembrance? Untrustworthy
    vision that it is: green fields variously
waving, gold fields variously waving,
    my friends variously waving, goodbye.

Don't talk about time to me. Any day
    in the life of the most retarded human
is worth a million years of stinking dinosaurs.
    Time to fill up a hole. Time to recall

whether this is a poor white trash paradise
        or a geriatric eden we're going to
so slowly and by such diverse, wandering routes.
        Now is good. The sky is filigreed, white

with ranges of mountainous cloud, and blue.
        It is all emotionless, as music is
inarticulate. Damn the anthropomorphic myths,
        the dead crutch of the sentimentalists.

Beautiful, emotionless, and serene
        as untroubled ignorance always is: Is knowledge
ever untroubled? Or is always to be serene
        a sign of mountainous stupidity?

Only a disappointed optimist
        could feel so bitterly towards the world as it is,
and love it as it might be, dreaming impossibilities,
        dreaming peace, dreaming green, dreaming knowledge

deeper than, than…than what? No oceans here,
        only bewilderment, a seeming momentarily
to understand overcome by squalid facts.
        The ocean, the ocean, what world is this?

Driving into Tampa, passing houses
        for sale, unbuilt except for their surrounding walls,
an alien flatness, heavy air, and one thinks of
        the person oppressed by the place. There is

the rotting smell of the Atlantic. Palms,
        brown, vaguely green, tufty, comical to a Northern eye,
routinely line the avenues. There should be swamps,
        but I see none. The oyster beds are dead.

There is no idea of order here,
    no key in the west of this peninsula,
this ramshackle, depleted yellow and brown
    where all are polite, soft-spoken, remote

in their disorganized fountain of youth.
    I seem to be the youngest here. They are waiting
for death to pounce, waiting in a remote way.
    The approach of death is so casual.

America is truly beautiful.
    We drove so many laps to come back home again.
This is home. This is home. Is this home?
    I damn drove all over America

to come back. The grass is greener somewhere.
    That was a summer place and this is an arctic place.
Hello mom. I've been good. But I drink too much
    and my friends' love is unacceptable.

The wolves are out in the sagging landscape
    and to come back and to come back is unacceptable.
All over America it was being a stranger
    of an acceptable variety

entranced me, never to come back to face
    any sort of reality in that land
of new castles and sea coasts and oysters
    and never any stranger knowing me.

Waiting for rainbows that never come in,
    trying to find a word in this absurd, absurd game;
it's comfortable, I guess. I wish I had a vision
    that would explain, or something beautiful.

Love is a silk thing people say, like God,
        or I adore my shoes, or where is the softest path?
Who can believe any of that? It's all talking.
        They put kool-aid in your cereal here.

And now Vancouver's gutters will be full
        of clumped, sodden cherry blossoms and, walking
through another sea-city, it seems as alien
    as the stranger places were in sunshine.

I'm going off course, plants are exploding
        all over the earth, bursting green, bursting red,
these are the locust years that come to everyone,
        coming to this speckled, dying planet,

this earth of luxury, forgetfulness,
        and defeat. What has its stark, jangling music
for me, engrossed with my trivial sorrows?
        I see heroes grazing in my garden.

This willful lack of will: I do know what
        I'm doing. I take risks too, as much as you
who have thrown away the past in disarray.
        Drunks get used to walking through everything,

including window panes and love, holding
        shells pressed to their ears, listening for the sound
of the day, the sea enveloping their swollen minds
        awash with failed dreams replaced by schemes

too transparent for tears, too ludicrous
        for laughter, wanting to lie down in the arms
of the day. It hurts: the shock of being normal. And who
        truly regards himself as exotic?

Loneliness drinks me. That's also a lie.
    I'm also tired of my cock falling in love,
of not knowing when someone loves me, not knowing
    what civilization I am part of.

You who lived desired and died lamented,
    the rubble of self-pity and frustration
still remains; but now for you there is no land
    uninhabitable. And, too, there is

nothing more to do but to let time have
    its way, to utter all the appropriate
sentences. The death chamber never empties:
    such a crowd! and such assiduity!

I'm having a difficult time, poem.
    Leave me alone and I'll tell you everything,
even the dumb things I make up, even poetry,
    even the truth. The truth! Who cares for that?

Everyone is wise. The idiot is
    a master in his idiocy and he
knows things he cannot explain to the others.
    We're just carriers for our genes anyway.

God only knows what they're up to tonight,
    those aids to eternity, to destiny,
manufacturing chaos into cosmos
    so that even I have observed myself

wrapped for a moment in the cold dark cloak
    of fate, always doubtful even of my own doubts.
How splendid, how pregnant, to feel persecuted,
    to be composed of vegetable peels.

How important it makes me in my own eyes.
We live in a land of loonies, where to say
I don't like means I don't understand, in which
the citizens are murderous and dumb

and here. It is always the others
who decide who we are, or will be, publicly.
We adapt to the disguises easily,
adopting or discarding the many-

coloured silk, minds easily treacherous
and flexible, stooping in humility,
dreaming revenge, justification, reply,
victory, and to be ourselves again.

Were we ever? There are those who will find
jobs but no comfort. Life being what it is,
we attempt to make our selves indiscernible.
Honesty is praised and left to shiver.

The soul is crystallized. And now it is winter
again. The snow will begin to fly, white lie,
another year has gone by and so few lines
written down and so many of them dreamed.

And another day closer to death, said
my father at breakfast. True enough but
a hell of a thing to say over coffee
and orange juice and eggs. But true enough.

I am killing time before time kills me.
Even I have deserved myself, silkily
skirting memory, which will not recall itself,
in favour of weather, whether or not

there is meaning in these dull mysteries.
    Most prospectors for gold find mud. Why should I
even want to be different? Klondike day
    of the soul! What fun! What gaiety! What

bullshit. There is a strange clear trembling band
    of interference across my vision. I
am a humourless and petulant baboon.
    Wah, wah, I hate you all. You all hate me.

This is just debris. This is you and me
    in love, out for a spree. If everyone my age
has the face he deserves then I don't know what
    I deserve, what any of us deserves.

Lord, give me the strength to see the angels
    moving in the confused welter of my life.
Do not let my eyes remain in this failing
    proportion to my loving heart always.

I could advance calmly toward my death
    if that were all. But there is still the green world
of those who love me, and whom I love, I do,
    but cannot tell. How sweet those flowers are!

We've never been sure of ourselves, have we,
    despite the beatings, despite the love, despite
governing our lives, being the only child
    moving into the green obscure forest

of emotion? It is this other thing.
    If sex were all then every doll could make us.
Squeak. Everything's water. If you look long enough
    it's all silk and plastic flowers. These are

not soliloquies in hell, or eden,
        but on earth, surrendered, raped, mutilated,
rained upon with acid and rage, stripped bare, buggered,
        filled with sand, spat upon by lepers, green.

What a childish lament frustration is.
        I ought to make pretty pictures but it is
always better to travel on. And wiser.
        Wiser. Let us swaddle our minds in silk,

you friends, you enemies, you lovers, you,
        this urge to be loved, to dependence, never
ceases....

From THE TASMANIAN DEVIL & OTHER POEMS, 1999

FIFTY-SEVENTH BIRTHDAY

I seem to be forgetting what words sound like.
Soon I shall be reduced to a tiny vocabulary of phrases
such as I love you,
or I hate you,
or death.

LOVE AFFAIR

I'm not in love with anyone, not even myself.
It's hard, living without hopelessness.

AN OLD MAN, WAITING

                                        in a chair,
growing old beyond repair,
watching his hands, the enlarging veins,
feeling his blood run slower, knows the pains
multiply, and the consequences of every lie
fade as people grow patienter
and more remote. To disinter
the past is easy and more inaccurate
than Now is. It is time to endure a pat,
dismissing, on the shoulder, missing
nothing and accepting all,
waiting for Eden, after the Fall.

AN EXAMINATION

Again the doctor's mechanical prodding:
When did your parents die,
and why? It's a pity your children
are not your own; we might have told

from their diseases the reasons
for your complaint. (I'm getting old;
that's complaint enough.) It hurts

when I do this? And this? And this?
(Yes. And that and that and that.)

Take these pills with every meal,
take these for pain as needed (I don't need
pain) and these before you sleep.

I cannot sleep. Are my children not my own?
Why *did* my parents die?

THE CAT

It is not epiphanies we are after
(God forbid!)
but a small truth or two –

the vinegar lakes, the excremental rivers,
the cancer fish, the grey-haired trees, the coughing birds
    at their song
    all summer long,
the place manipulating the people –

the world makes us what we want,
the world makes us want.

The cat
slouches off, out of the poem, sure of itself,
bored.
We make the world.

A PICTURE FROM AN EXHIBITION

The man on the exhibition ride,
seeking only gravity's thrill defied,
catapulted
down. It was not what he had meant.
Oh no he cried,
oh no he said softly, assaulted, insulted,
and as he lay on the cement
the world died.

IT'S WINTER IN OTTAWA

The streets are full of overweight corporals,
of sad grey computer captains, the impedimenta
of a capital city, struggling through the snow.

There is a cold gel on my belly, an instrument
is stroking it incisively, the machine
in the half-lit room is scribbling my future.

It is not illegal to be unhappy.
A shadowy technician says alternately,
Breathe, and, You may stop now.
It is not unreasonable to be unhappy.

HOME TOWN

This country is so old that no one can remember
its history. The sky blooms and the rocks flower.

Pacific, Atlantic, Arctic, Prairie. The oceans
surround us, blue, grey, white, green, the land

goes on forever.

Canada is my home town. Trees fill the mind
and people look at me sideways and smile.

A CARTOON

"Call it a weakness," says the witch,
  ducking her head coyly, like someone violently in love,
    as Bugs Bunny lectures her on the immorality
      – the sheer inutility –

of dining on children. She has become
  almost a young girl again, so shy,
    at being caught in self-indulgence,
      seeking forgiveness.

There is no forgiveness.

The Tasmanian Devil knows that.
  But he wants justice, or, at least, an answer.
    "Whyfor you bury me in the cold, cold ground?"
      he asks. And there is no answer.

Not even Bugs Bunny knows the answer to that one.

LIKE AN EEL

Hunting after myself in slightly used poems
is a heartbreaking chore. The past
is a foreign country and the quarry

is sly and elusive, a liar twisting
and twisting about the words like an eel
on a spear, dying, never to be known.

AN INSCRIPTION TO RICHARD JEFFRIES ON A SARSEN AT BARBURY

It is Eternity now.
I am in the midst of it.
It is about me
in the sunshine.

From GROUNDSWELL: THE BEST OF ABOVE/GROUND PRESS, 2003

THE DEATH OF THE HIRED MAN

He collapsed like a sack of wet shit,
which is what we all are, if you think of it,
and lay without a twitch in the deep pit
he had been ordered not to dig in that massive heat,
transformed into, as we all will be, a piece of meat.

"These Things Form Poems When I Allow It": After John Newlove

Jeff Derksen

A Long Continual Argument covers the forty years of John Newlove's publishing life, beginning with *Grave Sirs* in 1961, punctuated in 1972 with his Governor General's award winning *Lies*, shifting register with the long poem *The Green Plain* in 1979, and culminating with *The Tasmanian Devil & Other Poems* (1999) and the broadside edition of "The Death of the Hired Man" from 2001, his last published work before he passed away in Ottawa due to a brain hemorrhage. Given this timeframe, these carefully structured poems that make up *A Long Continual Argument* are nested within two parallel continual arguments – one literary and one social – that shape our readings of the poems and with which the poems are in direct dialogue.

The first continual argument I have in mind is the project of contemporary Canadian literature imagined as a formation integral to historically grounded, and contested, national identities and a larger national sense of self, a sort of national structure of feelings (to rescale Raymond Williams' term up to the national) correlated through literature. This continual process of defining a national literature has been uneven both in its development and its inclusions and exclusions, but the period that Newlove's publishing life covers is a particularly intense phase of development, contestation, and plasticity. Set alongside our present moment, it is not a time when literature or poetry mattered more, the "golden age" of CanLit, but a moment when texts were asked and imagined to do something very different than they can do now. Perhaps this is marked by a shift from a Canadian culture industry as a national project devised to shape a historical narrative that would define a place for Canada in the world system of nation states in the post-colonial moment to a Canadian cultural market that has more effectively collapsed the cultural into the economic, the national into the logic of the global, and the citizen into the logic of neoliberalism.

Secondly, over the last four decades there has been a gradual yet dramatic reshaping of Canadian society, within a globalized context, that has seen bedrock cultural and economic assumptions altered by both internal debates, and by external pressures and global harmonizations. While any author's selected works is a gathering of historical gestures and contexts, both textual and social, a collected works that spans four of the most slyly transformational decades of the long twentieth century is necessarily nested in and intertwined with the historical conditions. These conditions are not blunt nor even graspable in their totality, but are rippling with friction and conflict, as well as, in the case of *A Long Continual Argument*, moments of clarity, joy, disappointment, and resignation. Further, these moments cohere on a ground where individual identity and subjectivity are in an unstable relationship to the community and group (whether ethnic or racial community or the national imagined community) and the other (dramatically, comradely, and at times problematically in Newlove's work, First Nations and women).

It's useful, then, to acknowledge or even confront the fact that a selected or collected works, particularly a posthumous one, periodizes an author's work and I think it is necessary and rich to read the poetry while keeping in mind the cultural, social and aesthetic relationships it was produced within, in dialogue and reaction with. Two strains that I think arises throughout *A Long Continual Argument* are a dialogue with the cultural discourse of Canadian Literature and an address to, a disgust with, and a resignation to the shape of society and the fleeting joys and false openings an individual imagination conjures and hopes for. By reading this selected works as a periodizing of Newlove's poetry within these frames, I borrow from Fredric Jameson's notion of the "period" as "not some omnipresent and uniform shared style or way of thinking and acting, but rather as the sharing of a common objective situation, to which a whole range of varied responses and creative solutions is then possible, but always within the situation's structural limits" (178). The long continual argument of the title, is in fact a dialogue between these very "structural limits" that Newlove identifies, defines, and writes of and the "creative solutions" that are experienced, imagined, or shut down at various levels and places. Or, as the lines that Newlove ends the poem "Remembering Christopher Smart" with remark: "I see that we all make the world what we want. / Our disappointment lies in the world as it is." Here is the powerful intersection of limitations and expectations that generates the continued friction and precision of Newlove's work.

Given the frame of these two parallel arguments, the poems in *A Long Continual Argument* are simultaneously social registers of one person's life over forty-plus years – a register that shows a social imprint on consciousness and the body in sculpted, hard-edged lyrical poems that open to expressiveness through their precision – and poems that are part of the project of a national literature even as they are reflexive about that project. Specifically, the poems carry a reaction to and sometimes a resignation to – at a very subjective level – rural and small town life in Canada, the promise of cities and an urban life, the movement for jobs and love and kicks, the joys and difficulties of family life, as well as relations that we understand at a more abstracted level even though we experience them in very material and everyday ways – gender relations, class relations, and the relationship of history to how we locate ourselves, both collectively and individually, in the present. Poetically, and socially, there is also the tension of the imperative to find and speak your own "voice" (even if that voice is understood as part of a "national voice" of poetry or marked by a particular identity) within the relationship of the self to the other and within a bounded or even static space. This relationship of place, and of figure and ground, in Newlove's work is spatially complex with the various scales of space nested in one another, but with an event-filled liminal zone in between. For instance, country and city are joined or articulated in Newlove's poetry, but the liminal space between them is where a lot of the laconic action happens.

Likewise, the relationship of self and other is, in Newlove's work, dialogic, based on the recognition that one's own voice exists only in relationship to other voices. And, as is driven home in the poems in this selection, Newlove foregrounds the imbalance of power in this dialogic relationship: the voices of First Nations, of the historically repressed (and of repressed histories), of women, of the working class, of rural lives are all in tension and relation throughout this book. What is striking is that this tension is both personal (or intrapersonal, between people) and forged from pressures of the period and social relations. All of the people, places, things, bodies, and voices in these poems are *under* the heavy weight of the social and its reification, its alienation combined with minor moments when that alienation is punctured.

At times, this imbalance of power is brought sharply into focus and at other times these relations are reflected in the poems themselves. But, if we take the sixties as Jameson defines it, as the decade that ends around 1972-1974 (and I think this works for Canada, even if we consider the state crisis of the FLQ and the invocation of the War Measures Act as the end of a sixties), then the themes that Newlove continues to ruminate on and develop are all cued up by the time of his 1972 Governor General's winner, *Lies*. And the philosophical and social framework to examine these themes is also in place, and in alignment, I think, with "a significant and social *symptom*" of the long sixties, that Jameson marks as "in the mid-60s, people felt it necessary to express their sense of the situation and their projected praxis in a reified political language of power, domination, authority and antiauthoritarianism..." (184). But in the case of Newlove and of many of Canadian poets, this language was torqued or irritated to try to shatter the reification of language and experience, its ossification of the everyday, and the poetry aimed at recording the impact of the times on the subject, on the body, on voice, on identity, and more generally on place and history. In more avant-gardist positions, the fight is against the reification of language itself (understood materially or as a homology of the social). But Newlove strikes a balance between materiality and reification in his strongest poetry – thematically reflecting reification in everyday life and the relations between people (for reification is relational) while materially crafting poems which strain at reification by a tension of proximity and distance. The spatiality of the poems – the relationship of landscape to self, of the urban to the rural, and the event-horizon of the liminal spaces – plays out in this dialectic of proximity and distance at a subjective level.

This incomplete cataloguing of the concerns and conflicts that Newlove's poems grapple with can easily be organized – and given a thematic clarity – through the metaphors that Canadian Literature etched out to define its contours. But these categories, drafted to bring the nation into historical presence and spatial legibility – metaphors of survival, of a relationship to the landscape and to national space, to the necessity of national identity, and to a mytho-spatial poetics of a land with contested histories and malingering colonial relations – do not sit easily either with the jarring and unsettling aspects of the poems in *A Long Continual Argument* nor with the reflexive dialogue the poems have with the discourse of Canadian Literature. Even when I first read Newlove's "Ride Off Any Horizon" in *15 Canadian Poets* (before its expansion), and before I had the sense of Canadian poetry as a field itself, the poem seemed both bigger than the themes it was laying out, even as it was precise in its particularity: how could "any horizon" be a specific Canadian prairie horizon, was the horizon spatial or temporal, conceptual or material? This counter flow – of universalizing the particular, but not losing its particularity – somehow went against the current with the other poems in that anthology and created an irritating eddy. As a result, even though there is a general sense that the important, constitutional so to speak, work of Canadian Literature was done in this period, Newlove's poems resist such a clear-cut designation as, for instance "prairie poems" or categorization as engaged in the thematics of survival that was not a socially charged understanding of survival embedded into everyday practices. These poems are difficult to mollify into such reductions for three specific reasons: the poems are reflexive of – or one could say self-aware – of these literary categories and therefore alter the categories themselves rather than merely fitting in: the poems hammer away at a bleakness (reification played out as proximity and distance) that is driven home at the subjective not national scale; and, as I've suggested, the poems tell us more about the social relations (and class relations specifically) of an extended period and how they effect a view of the world than Canadian literature correlated as a thematic catalogue allows.

So, it is not possible to casually, yet accurately, write in an afterword for this collection that Newlove was a poet whose work helped define Canadian Literature during a time when it was taking a contingent yet dominant shape. To do so pushes aside the other scales that these poems work at – for the national scale is not the predominant one – and it also pushes aside the kind of affect registered in the poems, and tripped off by them in the reader. Newlove's place in the cultural field of Canadian literature is already established – and no doubt it will be enhanced and rethought with this volume – and poems such as "Ride off Any Horizon", "Samuel Hearne in Wintertime" "Crazy Riel", "The Pride" and "Veregin, Moving in Alone" take a position alongside the key poems of Canadian literature in which the representation of identity, place and history and the possibilities of poetic form and voice intersect to create insight and poetic possibilities. And in reading this collection now, it is the intersection of affect within historical conditions that equally drives the poems.

Poetic theories of affect can be seen as a means to resist an imagined reduction of literary texts to socio-political markers and return the poem to corporeal and aesthetic events that record or produce emotions. Yet to imagine affective emotions as separate from the truly affective social relations severs the poem from the two things – the imperatives of a literary history in the making and the material social and historical conditions of a period – that I have proposed as parallel arguments to *A Long Continual Argument.* It is tempting to look at this compilation of Newlove's poems as an affective gathering where Canadian landscapes give way to the blackness of night and the noir shadows of cities that fail to fulfill their promises (as in "The Cities We Longed For") – promises viewed from afar from small towns, farms, roadsides, or from liminal spaces such as street corners, rented apartments, and temporary domestic spaces. This tone is of a hard life broken by moments of brief happiness and surprising admissions of love that then turn to an ironic pulling away from love itself. Yet this tone of the poems is built both from Newlove's poetics – the careful syllabics, the precision of his line breaks (consider how the line break works in "Ride Off Any Horizon"), and what Robert Duncan memorably called the tone leading of vowels – and from the subject matter of the poems.[1]

Usefully, here is how Sianne Ngai, in her book *Ugly Feelings*, describes tone: "By 'tone' I mean a literary or cultural artifact's feeling tone: its global or organizing affect, its general disposition or orientation towards its audience and the world" (28). Ngai, is careful however, not to have tone rest at this emotive formal level, but she moves it to create a link between the poem and what I called above "the imperatives of a literary history in the making and the material social and historical conditions of a period". Ngai explains further: "Instead, I mean the formal aspect of a literary work that makes it possible for critics to describe a text as, say 'euphoric, or 'melancholic', and, what is much more important, the category that makes these affective values meaningful with regard to how one understands the text as a totality with an equally holisitic matrix of social relations" (28). A related way to look at this is to see tone as the aesthetic software that creates the interface between the literary text and the "holistic matrix of social relations", or how the poems, in their long continual argument, engage intellectually and affectively with the continual arguments they are embedded within.

Ngai focuses brilliantly and exclusively on "negative affects that read the predicaments posed by a general state of obstructed agency " (3) – ranging from envy to disgust – and I've already suggested that disgust is one of the reactions that the reader is drawn into in the works in this selected poems. But disgust here is a socially situated disgust, not a melancholy for possibilities, but a powerful intersection of limitations and expectations experienced across the Canadian social landscape – that is, the affects, the powerful emotional performance of these poems, come from "obstructed agency". And, as I'm suggesting, obstructed agency is often spatial in the poems – the sense of containment of small towns, the modernist trope of the isolated individual in the city, the nation as unknowable, even the isolation of lovers and the distance of one from ones own body (as in "An Examination"). Coincidentally, E.D. Blodget has proposed "the search for agency" as one of the periods that Canadian literary criticism moved through: here we can grasp the self-reflexive tension in Newlove's poems with this national literary criticism, for agency in his poetry is obstructed socially – or the potential of agency, the possibilities of agency, are continually moving from proximity to distance, hoped for but not graspable. Yet, the negative possibilities of agency, when it can be achieved, are also part of the landscape of these poems – this is shown as of the subjugation of another. So Newlove's poetry also reads about the constitution of agency and power across the Canadian social landscape.

Perhaps Newlove is a modernist poet of a belated Canadian modernism whose writing carefully catches the effects of modernization through the tropes of isolation, alienation, and social fragmentation. Certainly in the representations of the city, and of the administration of society (moving from a more tightened-down determined view to a deadly dry humorous take as in "It's Winter in Ottawa") this modernist view takes hold, but in Newlove's work it is not a general cultural condition, but the conditions of capitalism and the effects of wage labour (and its flip side, unemployment). This is how the long continuous argument with the social is felt throughout this selected works. That Newlove's last published poem is the devastating and ironic "The Death of the Hired Man" holds this up, but I don't want to argue that his work is universal in this way – catching a generalized structure of feeling of a period – because a reader is struck by the particularities in the poems (both imagistically and in tone). But I think we can also read Newlove's work as being caught on the cusp of what Jameson sees as the "waning of affect" and yet working through of what Ngai describes as "capitalism's classic affects of disaffection" (4). This complicated knot finds its way into a key poem, *The Green Plain* (a work that defies my categorizations in many ways), of Newlove's work and this stanza carries the oscillation of proximity and distance and the reverberation of tone that has made his work endure:

                                        always ignorant,
always amazed, always capable of delight,
and giving it, though ending in hatred, but
an image only. Of disaster. But there is no disaster.
It is just that we lose joy and die.

End Notes

1. I'm relegating a personal anecdote to an endnote (poetics reference: bpNichol "Friends as Footnotes"). In the early 1980s, I studied with John Newlove at the David Thompson University Centre in Nelson, B.C. DTUC was, in a way, a Canadian version of Black Mountain College, and later, after it was shut down in one of the early examples of the neoliberalisation of Canadian post-secondary education, DTUC gave a difficult birth to the Kootenay School of Writing which continues today in Vancouver. DTUC was a dynamic place to study and to *learn* how to be a writer, and one afternoon I recall Newlove asking me into his house as I dropped him off so he could show me the careful syllabics of an Irish writer (who I can't recall now), literally counting the syllables per line, noting their stress patterns (and the breaks and shifts in patterns).

Works Cited

E.D Blodgett Five Part Inventory: *A History of Literary History in Canada*. Toronto: U of Toronto P, 2003.

Jameson, Fredric. "Periodizing the 60s". *Social Text* 9/1 (Spring Summer 1984): 178-209.

_____. *Postmodernism, or, The Cultural Logic of Late Capitalism*. Durham: Duke UP, 1991.

Ngai, Sianne. *Ugly Feelings*. Cambridge, MA: Harvard UP, 2005.

INDEX OF TITLES

Alcazar 120
America 119
And the Dead Rose up from the Water 131
Apparition, The 123
Arrival, The 17
Autobiography 211
Autobiography 211
Autobiography 213
Autobiography 213
Autobiography 216
Before Sleep 115
Before the Big Bend Highway 19
Being Caught 208
Big Bend, The 96
Big Mirror 182
Birds, Dear, 15
Black Night Window 56
Blue Cow Phrases 166
By the Church Wall 43
By the Grey Atlantic 117
Cartoon, A 233
Cat, The 230
Cave, The 130
Cities We Longed For, The 176
Cold, Heat 189
Common Root, The 60
Company 138
Complaint 164
Concerning Stars, Flowers, Love, Etc. 181
Crab Apples, The 62
Crazy Riel 67
Crow Walking 144
Death of the Hired Man, The 236
Dog, The 63
Double-Headed Snake, The 76

Doukhobor 112
Dream 163
Dream 163
Driving 175
East from the Mountains 38
End Justifies the Means, The 16
Engine and the Sea, The 108
Every Muddy Road 132
Everywhere I Go 164
Examination, An 229
Fat Man, The 124
Fifty-Seventh Birthday 227
Film of Lhasa, A 79
First Bird of Spring, The 161
Five Poems After Sanskrit 194
Flower, The 107
Flowers, The 32
For Judith, Now About Ten Years Old 28
Four Small Scars 30
Funeral 23
Green Plain, The 170
God Bless You 117
God Bless the Bear 212
Gross Masks 146
Hero Around Me, The 133
Hitchhiker, The 66
Home Town 232
How the Weather Is 121
Indian Women 74
In Libya 31
In the Crammed World 167
In the Forest 40
Inscription To Richard Jeffries on a Sarsen at Barbury, An 235
Insect Hopes 191
It Is a City 147
It Was All There 80
It's Winter in Ottawa 231

Kamsack 37
Lady, Lady 81
Letter to Larry Sealey, 1962, A 45
Like a Canadian 88
Like a River 160
Like an Eel 234
Like Water 186
Long Continual Argument With Myself, A 169
Love Affair 228
Love Letter 48
Mirror, The 92
My Daddy Drowned 18
My Dreams 135
No Furniture for a Room 24
No Pleasure 148
No Song 87
North America 57
Not Moving 20
Notes From and Among the Wars 151
Nothing is to be Said 27
Old Man, The 65
Old Man, Waiting, An 228
Permanent Tourist Comes Home, The 178
Picture From An Exhibition, A 230
Poem with Ravens 214
Prairie, The 114
Pride, The 100
Progress 217
Public Library 83
Report on Absence 187
Remembering Christopher Smart 118
Return Train 186
Revenge 116
Ride Off Any Horizon 69
Rocks, Woods, Seas 180
Samuel Hearne in Wintertime 93
Shakespeare's Sonnets 190

She 149
Singing Head, The 35
Sky, The 134
Slow Spring 137
Solitaire 91
Speech About a Blackfoot Woman With Travois, Photo By R.H. Trueman 196
Squirrel Peanut Butter Song, The 89
Such Fun, Such Fun 215
Svejk 188
That's the Way Everything Is 49
Then, If I Cease Desiring 26
Three Days is Too Long 55
Two Letters from Austria 47
Until It Was Yellow 162
Vancouver Spring 50
Veregin 22
Veregin, Moving in Alone 52
Warm Wind 110
Weather, The 207
Well-Travelled Roadway, The 42
What Do You Want? 82
When I Heard of the Friend's Death 78
White Cat 25
White Lies 136
White Philharmonic Novels 197
Wind, The 111
Why Do You Hate Me? 165
You Cannot Step Twice 61
You Know 49
Yukichi Fukuzawa 185

ACKNOWLEDGEMENTS

The poems in this edition originally appeared in the following books and chapbooks:

Grave Sirs, Periwinkle Press, 1961.
Elephants, Mothers & Others, Periwinkle Press, 1963.
Moving In Alone, Contact Press, 1965, reprinted Oolichan Books, 1977.
Black Night Window, McClelland and Stewart, 1968.
The Cave, McClelland and Stewart, 1970.
Lies, McClelland and Stewart, 1972.
The Green Plain, Oolichan Books, 1981.
The Night the Dog Smiled, ECW PRESS, 1986.
Apology for Absence, The Porcupine's Quill, 1993.
The Tasmanian Devil & other poems, above/ground press, 1999.
GROUNDSWELL: the best of above/ground press, Broken Jaw Press, 2003.

Poems originally from *The Night the Dog Smiled* published with the permission of ECW Press.

Robert McTavish holds degrees in English (Simon Fraser University) and Journalism (University of Regina). He is a documentary filmmaker who has made several films with his company, Non-Inferno Media. He recently spent several years researching and preparing the documentary *What to make of it all? The life and poetry of John Newlove.*

Jeff Derksen is a poet and critic who works at Simon Fraser University. Derksen's critical writings on globalization and culture, poetry, architecture, and art have been published extensively in North America and Europe. His most recent book of poetry is *Transnational Muscle Cars* (Talon, 2003), preceded by *Dwell* (1994) and *Down Time* (1990) which won the 1991 Dorothy Livesay Poetry Award at the BC BookPrizes. He collaborates, under the name Urban Subjects with the artists Sabine Bitter and Helmut Weber on projects regarding urbanism and globalization.

Other titles from Chaudiere Books

Collected Sex. Poetry anthology, rob mclennan, editor. 978-0-9781601-8-0
Decalogue: ten Ottawa poets. rob mclennan, editor. 978-0-9781601-3-5
Decalogue2: ten Ottawa fiction writers. rob mclennan, editor. 978-0-9781601-4-2
Disappointment Island. Monty Reid, poetry. 978-0-9781601-1-1
Everything is Movies. Nicholas Lea, poetry. 978-0-9781601-7-3
Movements in Jars. Meghan Jackson, poetry. 978-0-9781601-0-4
Old Winter. Anne Le Dressay, poetry. 978-0-9783428-0-7
The Desmond Road Book of the Dead. Clare Latremouille, fiction. 978-0-9781601-2-8
The Ottawa City Project. rob mclennan, poetry. 978-0-9781601-6-6
There Is No Mountain : Selected Poems of Andrew Suknaski. Andrew Suknaski, poetry. rob mclennan, editor. 978-0-9781601-5-9